● Report

"Forgive Us Our Debts":
lending and borrowing as
if relationships matter

Nathan Mladin and Barbara Ridpath

Commendations

"This short book is an excellent introduction to Christian thinking about debt, whether personal, business or sovereign. It is comprehensive, covering the basic background facts, biblical teaching, theological insights from the church fathers through to contemporary approaches, and developing a framework to address contemporary challenges. Its broad approach should be welcomed by Christians from differing theological and political perspectives. It offers distinct policy recommendations, with which some will certainly disagree, but because of this, is a good basis for an extended conversation on the subject. It deserves to be read widely."

Lord Griffiths of Fforestfach, Chairman, Centre for Enterprise, Markets and Ethics

"This report engages with the issue of debt thoughtfully and thoroughly from a Christian perspective. It makes clear how the power of debt can shape relationships, positively as well as negatively. It avoids simplistic moralising, and it points out ways ahead. I am delighted to recommend it."

Rt Hon Stephen Timms MP, former Chief Secretary to the Treasury

"The topic of finance and money has long been a taboo subject in society, including within the Church. We hope this report will prove helpful in enabling Christians to explore their beliefs and open up healthy discussion that will boost the sense of a support network for those who are struggling."

Matt Barlow, CEO, Christians Against Poverty

Contents

Acknowledgements	5
Executive summary	7
Introduction	14
1 **Debt today: an overview of personal, corporate and public debt in the UK**	18
2 **Debt yesterday: debt, interest and usury in Christian thought**	47
3 **Debt tomorrow: lending and borrowing as if relationships matter**	79
Appendix	109
Glossary	117

Acknowledgements

Acknowledgements

On behalf of Theos and St Paul's Institute, we would like to thank the generous funders who enabled us to work on this project to produce this report: The Kirby Laing Foundation, The Fairfield Trust, Bruderhof, The Golden Bottle Trust, Hymns Ancient & Modern, Panahpur, James Perry, Antonio Batista, Robert Hughes-Penney, and John Langlois.

As part of our research we held two roundtables, one on personal debt, and the other on corporate and public debt. Both conversations, held under Chatham House rule, were stimulating and have informed this report. We are grateful to all those who participated – representatives of the debt advice sector, money and economics charities and think tanks, relevant public bodies, industry experts, academics and others.

We are also grateful to Prof Deborah James and Dr Ryan Davey, who hosted us at the LSE for a joint event where we were able to present some of our work.

Nathan would particularly like to thank Prof Luke Bretherton for giving up his time for a very stimulating phone conversation in the middle of the project, and for his excellent work on the theology of debt, which has richly informed the thinking that has gone into this report.

Barbara is particularly grateful to Bishop Peter Selby, "who taught me so much about the theology of money and finance."

Finally, we would both like to thank our colleagues at Theos, Bible Society, and St Paul's Institute, particularly Nick Spencer, Jodi Kiang, Katie Harrison, Lizzie Stanley, Canon Tricia Hillas, Paul Williams, and others who offered encouragement, advice, and invaluable support throughout.

Executive summary

Debt has always been with us.[1] In recent years, however, debt has changed considerably. It is now ubiquitous in our inter-dependent economies and has reached unprecedented levels across the world, the UK being no exception. This raises not only questions of sustainability, but more fundamental ones, such as, what kind of society do we want to be? And how do we want to distribute the risks and responsibilities that debt entails?

In this report, we examine personal, corporate and public debt in the UK and discuss the main areas of concern within a theologically informed moral framework. While much of what we say holds universally, our facts and examples have been taken from the UK. Below is a bullet point summary of the main findings, applications and recommendations resulting from our research.

Debt today

The economic facts

- Economic debt exists on three distinct yet interdependent levels: personal/household, business/corporate, public/government.

- The UK's economy is increasingly dependent on consumer growth, which is to a growing extent fed by debt.

- Personal debt has continued to increase since the Second World War, particularly after the financial crisis of 2008/9. As of 2017, total outstanding personal debt is equivalent to around 90% of the country's Gross Domestic Product (GDP).

- Today, 16 million British people have less than £100 in savings. Debt plays an increasing part in day to day spending. Many people borrow simply to cope with life events, such as job loss, divorce or illness, or in order to meet their basic needs.

— Government borrowing is at wartime levels. The combination of an increasing role for the state, increasing costs of service provision and a changing demographic profile of the country is leading to significant choices that need to be made between higher tax, lower provision of services or growing government debt.

— There is a severe lack of real investment by the private and public sector in the UK economy. This has led to an increased dependence on consumer spending and consumer borrowing for growth, and is diminishing the prospect of productivity growth and wage increases.

The moral issues

— Who bears the risks and responsibility for the repayment of debt is a moral question and a matter of political decision, rather than simply a technical or 'technocratic' one.

— Corporate shareholders are taking short-term profits at the expense of other stakeholders, notably the employee and the consumer.

— Government deficits are a moral issue on account of the principle of intergenerational equity and the question of how the burden of the deficit reduction is to be shared.

Debt yesterday

— Lending and borrowing are accepted practices in the Bible but regulated with a view to prevent abuses and exploitation, and to ensure all are able to participate in the common life.

— Interest is morally ambivalent in Scripture.

- There is a strong emphasis on debt forgiveness and lending as a form of gifting, particularly to those who are in distress.

- The Bible emphasises the individual responsibility of lenders and borrowers. It also recognises and regulates against systemic injustice.

- Throughout Christian history, up to the modern period, usury was consistently prohibited. A concern for the dignity and welfare of people, particularly the poor, lay behind the ban. For much of this period, interest and usury were basically interchangeable. It was only later that usury came to refer, as it does today, to extortionate levels of interest.

- Responding to developments in the wider cultural landscape, Christian theologians began to distinguish between usury and legitimate interest, and between commercial loans and loans made to the poor in times of distress.

- The ethical appraisal of debt became more sophisticated with time, yet there was never any compromise on the principle that economic relations are subordinate to social relations, and that money and profit should not crowd out moral and relational considerations in creating a common life.

Debt tomorrow

A moral framework

- Rather than dismissed wholesale or accepted uncritically, debt should be assessed in terms of its purpose, quantum or amount, and the effects it has on human social relations and, indirectly, to the physical environment.

- The Christian ethic put forward in this report sees debt as just or equitable when:

  - it is mutually beneficial to creditor and debtor;
  - risks associated with the contract are fairly distributed;
  - it can be shown to foster rather than corrode relationships – among debtors, creditors and all third-parties involved;
  - it enables participation in, rather than isolation from the common life;
  - it does not overburden future generations;
  - it is based on a responsible, steward-like relationship to the physical world.

A way forward

- How debt burdens are distributed between individuals, businesses and the government is a moral question and a matter of political decision. There needs to be appropriate public consultation and participation in the decision-making process on this issue.

- Deciding where to draw the lines of relationship and community – who is in, who is out, and on what basis – will be critical in re-establishing the relational nature of debt.

- If we are to see fair debt relations, lenders must understand the borrower's circumstances – not just their credit score. Borrowers, similarly, must be able to understand the terms of their debts. This presupposes necessary information is made available and accessible to both parties.

- New ways of ensuring risk is equitably shared must be devised. The disproportionate power institutional lenders have over individual borrowers must continue to be counterbalanced through appropriate regulation.

— Economic models should incorporate 'externalities' such as ecological damage to a greater extent than many currently do.

— A position of intergenerational equity may be achieved when debt is taken on to help create or enhance the conditions for the thriving of future generations: investment in health, education, disease-control, infrastructure etc.

— The concept of bankruptcy is an outworking of the Christian principle of debt forgiveness. As a society we need to continue to remove the stigma that still attaches to having to declare bankruptcy or apply for an Individual Voluntary Agreement (IVA).

— Better access to fair loans for the poor should not replace charity in the form of charitable debt forgiveness, grants and other forms of gifts.

This report ends with a series of general recommendations and practical applications to address the problematic features of contemporary debt in the UK. These are grouped according to what they seek to achieve: *formation*, which includes but is not limited to education (of both borrowers and lenders); better *communication* between borrowers, lenders, third parties and the wider society on debt issues; *mitigation* against harmful and problematic debt relations; and *reformation* of the debt economy.

1 See David Graeber, *Debt: The First 5000 Years* (London: Melville House, 2014 edition); Marcel Mauss, *The Gift: Forms and Functions of Exchange and Archaic Societies* trans. Ian Cunnison (Glencoe, Ill.: Free Press, 1954); Michael Hudson, *...and forgive them their debts: lending, foreclosure and redemption from Bronze Age Finance to the Jubilee Year* (Dresden: ISLET-Verlag, 2018).

Introduction

Introduction

Debt is one of the most pressing and complex issues of our age. It stretches from the world of geopolitics to that of personal and household budgets. It is a significant force in, and entrenched feature of, the life of individuals, families, businesses and countries today. People's views on debt vary widely according to upbringing, cultural norms and the demographic of the borrower and lender – as well as their views on the free market and capitalism.

This report is the culmination of a year-long research project undertaken by Theos and St Paul's Institute. Taking a holistic approach, it reviews debt in the UK at the personal/household, corporate/business and public/government levels, and offers a discussion of the main areas of concern within a moral framework derived from Christian theology. While much of what we are saying holds universally, our examples, facts and figures are taken largely from the UK.

Narrowly, debt refers to what a borrower must repay their lender. This can be broken down into the principal (the original amount lent) and the interest. It also refers to the social and economic practice of borrowing and lending more generally. Because it is ultimately a form of social interaction, all debt has an ineradicable moral dimension. It rests on implicit or explicit moral judgements about what is fair and good for individuals, institutions and the wider society about how different human beings relate to one another (and to the environment in which they operate). There are debt relations that clearly harm individuals and communities (e.g. payday loans with excessive interest that trap people into debt), and others that contribute, directly or indirectly, to their wellbeing (e.g. debt incurred for the purpose of productive investment).

Debt cannot be properly understood, let alone explained away, within a purely technical paradigm and vocabulary (e.g. contract, utility maximisation etc.). It must be analysed not only in terms of its ability to increase wealth and productivity, which it can and often does, but also in terms of the quality of relationships it establishes, with others and with the physical environment, and the way it enables – or hinders – meaningful participation in community and society more broadly.

These moral and relational dimensions of debt are often overlooked in contemporary debate. This report seeks to remedy this by putting forward a theologically informed moral framework for assessing contemporary debt and debt relations.

Chapter 1 (written by Barbara Ridpath) offers a primer on debt. It explains and reviews the features and salient issues around personal/household, corporate/business and public/government levels. Primarily descriptive, the chapter also begins to point towards the key areas of concern that warrant discussion within an ethical framework.

Chapter 2 (written by Nathan Mladin) consists of three main sections. The first is a biblical theology of debt, lending and borrowing, usury and interest. The second section is a brief historical theology of debt, surveying the Patristic period, the Middle Ages, and the Reformation. There is a particular focus on the moral evaluation of the practice of usury, which highlights some of the ethical concerns we deem important in the contemporary public debate on debt. The final section outlines three contemporary theologies of debt: the first from the Jubilee Centre, a Christian think tank based in Cambridge, UK; the second, the relationship between debt and gift found in the theological economics of Yale theologian Kathryn Tanner;

and, finally, the theology of debt articulated by theologian Luke Bretherton of Duke University.

Chapter 3 (co-written by Nathan and Barbara) begins by acknowledging the polyphony of views on debt but then seeks to bring out the principal melody within the broad Christian teaching on debt. This, we argue, comprises: the concern for the welfare of people, particularly the poor and marginalised; the ability of all to participate meaningfully in a common life; and the focus on justice and right relations between people, and between people and the physical environment. In the first part of Chapter 3 we put forward a moral framework for assessing contemporary debt in the UK, drawing on the theological and moral thought surveyed in Chapter 2. The second half of the chapter then identifies the key questions and areas of concern that emerged in Chapter 1 and brings the ethical teaching and moral categories to bear on the pressing issues around personal, corporate and public debt. Most of the issues covered emerged during the two roundtable conversations organised as part of this research project, which included academics, practitioners and representatives of relevant public bodies and the money and debt advice sectors.

In the final part of Chapter 3 we put forward a series of recommendations and concrete steps to be taken by individuals, public and private bodies, regulators and policy makers to address some of the ethically problematic features of modern debt at the personal, corporate and public levels. The recommendations are grouped around their specific focus area and the change they seek to achieve: *formation*, *communication*, *mitigation* and *reformation*. The report ends with an Appendix, which covers several of the theological and philosophical issues relevant to the topic of debt in a bit more detail, and a Glossary.

1
Debt today: an overview of personal, corporate and public debt in the UK

What is debt?

Debt is an amount of money borrowed by one person or entity from another. Many individuals, corporations and governments use debt to make purchases that they could not afford under normal circumstances. Most debts are expected to be repaid to the lender over time, along with an additional percentage of the amount borrowed (known as interest) for the use of this money.

This chapter looks at debt at the personal, business and national level, giving readers background on the nature of these obligations, their size and growth over time. This background will inform a review of the implications of debt, with an emphasis on what these contractual obligations do for those who bear the obligations, as well as the relational, societal and intergenerational implications of these obligations. Chart 1 puts these debts in the United Kingdom in historical context and demonstrates the relative size of each component:

Chart 1

Total UK Indebtedness (£billions)

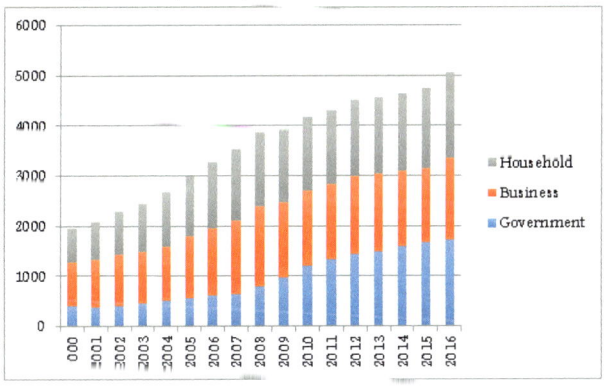

Source: Bank for International Settlements Statistics

The distinctions among the types of debt discussed are to a large extent artificial. Who bears the weight of debt and its repayment, whether the public, private or personal sector, is largely based on policy choices made by government and the private sector. Here are just a few examples:

— Are education, health and retirement privately or publicly funded?
— Is major national infrastructure, such as utility and transportation networks, in private or public ownership?
— Do incomes provided by employment or supplemented by the government permit all inhabitants to feed, clothe and house themselves on their income?

It can be helpful to think about debt as a giant game of 'pass the parcel' to see who will end up bearing the costs of the spending of others. However, the answers to these questions are largely a function of each person's ideology. There is no neutral, nor absolutely correct answer. In the recent past, the United Kingdom has seen the onus of retirement provision shift from the employer to the employee; we have seen a shifting share of corporate profits go from employee to the shareholder. Utilities have moved from largely public ownership to private ownership since the 1980s. Student debt funding has moved from a direct government expense to mostly at the student's expense. Each of these changes shifts funding – and often debt – from one segment of the economy to another. The rest of this chapter will explore the definition, nature and growth of these obligations, their implications and the interdependence among them.

Personal debt

There is little doubt that for as long as people have had access to money, they have simultaneously sought access to more money than they possess. This section will attempt to spell out the nature of personal debt, its impact on those who borrow and the larger economy. The second half of Chapter 3 addresses potential actions to tame the most pernicious abuses from the perspective of both the borrower and the lender.

> There is little doubt that for as long as people have had access to money, they have simultaneously sought access to more money than they possess.

A short history of problem debt resolution

Individual debt can have a sinister side, with personal borrowing having perilous consequences for those in Britain (particularly those from less-affluent backgrounds, who get on the wrong side of it). In Britain the phrase 'debtor's prison' has entered the common vernacular as a by-word for an individual being in a punitive and shameful state of penury. In previous centuries, doing a stint in one of these prisons was a common experience for many who could not pay back their creditors, with some – such as London's Marshalsea prison (whose notable former inmates included the father of author Charles Dickens) – being notorious for ensuring debtors could do nothing to improve their situation once they were inside. If friends and family did not come to an inmate's aid, then they could easily perish from starvation. It wasn't until the Debtors Act of 1869 that courts were prevented from imprisoning people for debt, except in special circumstances. The introduction of the Bankruptcy Act in 1883 reduced significantly the number of people being sent to prison for debt-related reasons.[1]

Despite incarceration being a counterproductive way to punish those who got into debt, prisons continued to hold people who had committed such offences until the early 20th century. Access to credit for ordinary people slowly started to expand via the founding of Friendly Societies, organisations that provided mutual financial benefits for members in the form of cooperative banking or insurance.[2] Building societies, first formed in the 18th century, also allowed their members to pool funds in order to pay for housing for themselves and other members, which in turn served as collateral to bring in further funds, allowing for more construction. These developments meant ordinary working people without access to banks could gain credit.[3]

Traditionally, credit was only readily available to those with sufficient wealth or income not to need it. Such borrowers used debt as a smoothing mechanism during their life cycle. They were young, net borrowers, buying their first cars and homes with loans and mortgages. As their incomes increased, they became net savers, repaying debts incurred earlier. In the later stages of their lives, they became net consumers of savings after retirement. While some people still follow that pattern today, the ways by which people accrue personal debt have changed considerably since the late 1960s, as have the reasons behind

> Traditionally, credit was only readily available to those with sufficient wealth or income not to need it.

getting into debt – and indeed the amount of debt too. More people have access to credit than ever before in the United Kingdom. Products, pricing and ways to differentiate among types of borrowers permit people of even modest means to obtain a loan of some sort. Wider access to credit has fuelled demand for such products, as has an emphasis on consumer consumption, and an 'I want it now' culture. Unfortunately, this can lead some to take on types of loans that are ill-suited to them, or amounts their levels of income will never permit them to repay. In this context, debt may also include amounts owed but not paid on time, known as arrears, on taxes or other payments, particularly local council taxes.

Traditionally, credit was used for major purchases such as homes, automobiles and sometimes major domestic appliances. Over time, the availability of short-term credit through credit cards led to borrowing for more short-term consumption: furniture, clothing, electronic equipment and Christmas gifts, wherever current income was insufficient to meet perceived current needs. The economic crisis of 2008 cost jobs and cut incomes. Combined with subsequent government moves to reduce spending, known as austerity policy (see Glossary), household income growth has stagnated at the lower levels of the income spectrum. In turn, this has pushed many households to borrow simply in order to be able to pay their utility bills such as gas, water and electricity and to buy basic food and clothing.

Moreover, the economy of the United Kingdom is increasingly dependent on the consumer for growth. The country's production

Debt-fuelled spending is the engine for economic growth in the current economy of Great Britain and many other developed countries.

is divided between manufacturing, services and agriculture. The flip side of the production coin is who uses what we produce. Uses include domestic consumption, net exports (i.e. people outside the UK consume it) and investment. Over time, UK investment has declined as a share of gross domestic product (GDP), while consumption has replaced it. This puts the government in an awkward situation regarding debt; unless ways can be found to spur productive long-term investment, if consumers do not spend, the economy does not grow.[4] This makes it relatively difficult for government policy to discourage personal borrowing and encourage savings. Current interest rate policy (see below) also strongly encourages increasing debt at the expense of savings. Debt-fuelled spending is the engine for economic growth in the current economy of Great Britain and many other developed economies.

Chart 2

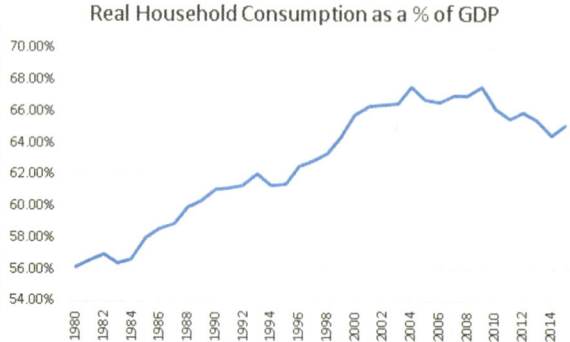

Real Household Consumption as a % of GDP

In order to think about the issue of household debt, it is important to consider how to best measure the changes in household debt and how to define when it threatens individual or national wellbeing. There are myriad measures of levels of indebtedness, both useful and misleading. In 1966 household debt to GDP, or the sum of all economic activity in the country, stood at nearly 58%.[5] This is a somewhat misleading measure, however, as it is comparing the total stock of personal debt to the flow of income in the economy. Throughout the 1970s and the first half of the 1980s debt levels in UK households decreased, staying consistently at 30–35% of the country's GDP. This rose to 60% in the early 1990s, 80% in the early 2000s and reached a high of 97% in 2010. As of 2017, the stock of outstanding personal debt, including home mortgages, consumer credit and credit card debts, was equivalent to around 90% of the country's GDP.[6]

As a percentage of disposable household income, or the income available to a family with which it must live, save and pay off its debt, personal debt was around 85% in 1987, rising from 93% in 1997 to 120% in 2001 and 157% in 2008. This too misleads, as households usually have a series of loans outstanding with different due dates, making it very unlikely that all household debt would become due and payable at once. Between 2016 and 2017, debt levels compared with household incomes increased rapidly from 133% to 140%. In absolute terms, private household debt saw an increase from £16bn to £47bn between 1980 and 1989.[7] Each of these measures is illustrative, and any used out of context can mislead. Nonetheless, the overall trend of each of these measures is clear: personal debt has continued to increase since the Second World War.

Increases in debt levels from the late 1980s to the present day were due to downturns in the economy, which led to an inability to manage debt on the part of many households (especially regarding mortgage repayments). The recession of the early 1990s resulted in many homeowners experiencing 'negative equity', where the value of their homes often fell below the amount borrowed in order to pay for them. Many who did not have their homes repossessed often ended up being in arrears with their mortgage payments by six months or more.[8]

It is important, however, when analysing these trends, to consider the distinction between borrowing for what might be described as 'productive use' versus borrowing for the sake of consumption. The former leaves you with an asset that has value at the end of the loan, while the latter tends to leave the borrower with nothing to show for it. Home mortgages fall in the first category, while credit cards and personal loans are often considered in the latter. Car loans and car leases fall somewhere in the middle.[9] Student loans, while unsecured, are considered as adding to 'human capital' and may increase the earnings power of the borrower upon receipt of the resulting education. (See more on this in the text box on student debt.) The distinctions between secured and unsecured borrowing are outlined in the text box below.

Secured versus unsecured debt

— The key difference between secured and unsecured debt is collateral – secured debt has some form of asset or property such as a house, a car or a computer behind it, put up by the borrower, as surety for the loan. In the event of a default, the proceeds of the sale of the asset would be used by the borrower to pay off the loan, with any residual monetary amount returned to the borrower. One such common example is mortgages.[10]

— The risk of loss for the party doing the lending is low in cases of secured debt, so long as the asset is appropriately valued and the loan is less than the full value of the asset the borrower is offering as collateral. In addition, as the borrower has to make a significant down payment on the loan, which he or she would lose on default, there is a strong incentive to continue to make payments. Lenders have a right to reclaim the asset (such as a car or house) if the borrower defaults on their payments. The borrower has a lot more to lose individually if she or he neglects their financial obligation, as the lender can take the asset and, in many cases, continue to chase the borrower for any unmade payments not met by the value of the collateral. Even so, the lender can ultimately lose the most, should it lend to too many borrowers who are unable to repay in an economic downturn. This suggests that, at a micro level, there is an asymmetry of risk between a commercial lender and a borrower. However, were a lender to extend credit to too many borrowers of similar characteristics (geography, income, quality of property), the lender itself could also be at risk.

— Interest rates are often lower on secured than unsecured loans. Lenders usually require borrowers to take steps to ensure the asset in question is protected, e.g. getting insurance for a house or a car.

— At the end of a secured loan, the borrower becomes the outright owner of the asset.

— Unsecured debt has no collateral to back it up. This means that if a borrower defaults on their payments then the lender often has to take legal action in order to obtain the money.

- A borrower's income and an estimation of the borrower's credit worthiness is the main way a lender can be sure they will be likely to pay back an unsecured loan. Banks will demand proof of a good credit score – based on historical payment of bills and repayment of credit – as a precursor to accessing these sorts of loans. They will charge a higher rate of interest where they perceive the likelihood of repayment to be weak. Banks will often require access to the client's main bank account data to lend in this way, with interest and repayments made by direct debit from that account.

- Outside of bank loans, common forms of unsecured debt include credit cards, which charge considerable rates of interest in exchange for issuing consumers with revolving lines of credit with no collateral backing.[11] A revolving line of credit means that a borrower can re-borrow the funds once they are repaid, as opposed to a one-off loan, which, once repaid, is not renewable. Those with poor credit records can often only access unsecured debt at very high rates of credit; rates lenders believe necessary based on the statistical risk of default by such customers.

While nominal interest rates[12] have declined markedly since the 2008 financial crisis (which has made borrowing less expensive), many households' financial wellbeing has suffered since the crisis because of stagnant nominal wage levels and changes in benefit payments that have added up to declines in real income for much of the population. These households have had the choice to decrease their standard of living or to borrow to maintain their standard of living. In the most severe cases, borrowing is needed simply to pay utilities such as gas, electric and water, and necessities such as food and clothing.

As we have already seen, there are indications that personal debt levels are reaching unsustainable levels. Much personal debt is variable rate, which means that the rate the borrower must pay changes with prevailing interest rates in the economy. So any increase in current interest rates from historical lows will have a dramatic effect on consumers' ability to repay, particularly without a concomitant increase in real wages. This is why the Bank of England and the Financial Conduct Authority (FCA) are so concerned about debt levels, as they limit their discretion to raise interest rates without significant repercussions.[13]

There are indications that, even at current low interest rates, debt burdens are becoming unaffordable for many. Applications for Individual Voluntary Arrangements (IVAs), a way for people to restructure personal debt, have risen to their highest level since they were introduced in 1987. StepChange, a national charity that helps individuals restructure their debt and improve their budgeting, received 620,000 requests for help in 2017, an all-time high. Personal loans, credit cards and car finance have risen higher than the rise in earnings by five times.[14]

Chart 3[15]

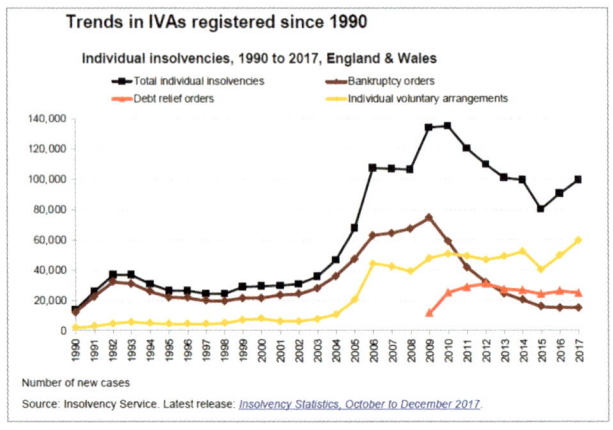

Student debt

Until 2006/07 university education in the United Kingdom was free to students (the costs were paid out of tax revenues). In the lead up to the change, maintenance grants, which had previously been given to students for living expenses, were gradually shifted to student loans. Government funding for the whole of student university costs became an increasing burden as the percentage of university-age population attending university grew from 5% to 35% in the last 50 years. When the tuition fees were introduced, students began to pay up to £3,000 per year – regardless of the university they attended. In 2012/13, this was raised to up to £9,000 a year, with most universities opting to move directly to the maximum fee.

To finance tuition fees, the existing student loan programme was increased to ensure financing from the government for tuition and some maintenance would be made available. Graduates begin repaying debt upon graduation when they earn in excess of £25,000 a year. Interest is paid at a rate of interest equivalent to the retail price index, the annual rate of increase in retail prices. Interest rates ratchet up as graduate earning levels increase. Repayment of the outstanding balance must be repaid at a rate of 9% of the borrower's income above the threshold rate of income of £25,000.[16]

This change led to £13 billion in student loans lent in 2017. The outstanding amount of student debt is expected to reach over £100 billion in 2018.[17] This has led to the average debt among the first major cohort of post-2012 students to become liable for repayment of £32,000.[18]

This shift in the financing of higher education to the individual student places a remarkable debt burden on young wage earners, reducing their ability to consume and most notably making it much more difficult to save the deposit necessary to consider property purchase. There are arguments both that this is depressing consumption and economic growth, and that there is a significant intergenerational transfer from millenials to middle-age, middle-class tax payers. The argument hinges on whether society or the student is the beneficiary of the education. It is clear that British society needs the expertise that comes with education to innovate, compete and thrive in the 21st century. However, it is also clear that the individuals are the chief financial beneficiaries of this policy, as most will attain significantly higher lifetime earnings as a result of their education than those who do not attend university. The income threshold permits people working in sectors with relatively low wages to be sheltered from debt repayment. To the extent the population is concerned about national indebtedness (see p. 40), it needs to make choices on where and how to spend tax revenue. In a society where there are limits on what voters will pay in tax, there are choices to be made about which segments of the population will benefit from tax redistribution and those who will pay for such redistribution.

Student loans illustrate the issue of burden shifting between government, businesses and individuals. They clearly demonstrate the national choices to be made and the trade-offs between an individualistic approach to financial indebtedness and a common good approach.

The explosion of types of credit, some regulated by the FCA and some not, complicates the picture, particularly for the unsophisticated borrower. Five years ago, the Church of England struck out at the lending practices of the payday lenders, such as Wonga (now in administration), as taking advantage of some of the poorest and most vulnerable in society with extortionate interest rates and conditions. The payday lenders, however, did understand that existing lenders and the regulation they had to follow often made the process and contracts more complicated than the borrower could understand well. Payday lenders also grasped the exigencies of getting to the end of the month for many borrowers and offered relatively small amounts of immediate cash. They solved an urgent problem for the client. However, in the process, they actually further impoverished the borrowers and often led them into a difficult cycle of borrowing in order to pay interest.

In 2015 interest rates were capped at 0.8% of the principal balance daily, but the Financial Ombudsman Service (FOS) received 10,529 new complaints about short-term credit providers in the 2016/17 financial year, a rise of 3216.[19]

In addition to payday lenders, hire purchase and instalment sellers, particularly of appliances, mean that the least able to pay end up paying most for a product, where the overall price includes the high effective rate of finance for that appliance.

Implications

How to think ethically about personal indebtedness will be discussed in Chapter 2 and 3. At this stage, it is important to reflect on how personal indebtedness can affect the economy. At sustainable levels of indebtedness, borrowing can spur consumption and national economic growth. However, overreliance on borrowing to consume makes the country susceptible to economic downturns, should households cut back on spending if they need to keep up with debt repayments. This can happen as interest rates rise, and could have negative implications on growth, and in turn unemployment, for the wider economy.

Banks' own profitability and solvency are placed at risk too, if they lend to individuals who default on their loans. Although mortgage debts are much larger, people are less likely to renege on their mortgage repayments. (However, in a sharp housing price decline, when homeowners are in a negative equity situation [this was the case in the early 1990s], they will sometimes just return the house keys to the lender.) As evidenced in the global financial crisis in 2008, banking collapse can have wide-ranging consequences for both the economy and its citizens.

Perhaps for this reason, the Bank of England has more recently expressed unease about the current state of mortgage lending and, in June 2017, issued guidelines about how mortgage lenders should carry out 'affordability checks' on those seeking to borrow.[20] Lenders will have to test whether homeowners could keep up with their mortgage repayments if they were required to pay an interest rate three percentage points above the lender's current standard variable rate.[21] This is because even a small change in interest rate on a large principal balance can be unaffordable if people's incomes are not also rising. This will make it a bit harder for people to get mortgages if it would involve really stretching their finances, but stops short of forbidding people from taking out loans per se.

> **16 million British people have less than £100 in savings and short-term borrowing is occurring to help those at the poorest income levels cope with life events such as job loss, divorce or illness, or to meet basic needs.**

The third consideration is what is making people need to borrow. Were it purely a desire for more goods and services the issue would centre on the rise of consumerism. However, 16 million British people have less than £100 in savings[22] and short-term borrowing is occurring to help those at the poorest income levels cope with life events such as job loss, divorce or illness, or to meet basic needs. Since the financial crisis, incomes have stagnated or fallen for those at lower income levels. This complicates any solution, and requires a national conversation on societal responsibilities, pay and benefit levels and appropriate levels of income distribution. As will be evident in the future section on national debt, such a discussion is deeply intertwined with national tax and debt policy.

Personal debt represents only a portion of total debt in the United Kingdom (see Chart 1), but choices among personal, business and national debt are strongly dependent upon policy decisions. In addition, outcomes are heavily interdependent, i.e.

a decrease in debt in one area can lead to increased indebtedness in another. To understand the full picture, we need to look at debt borrowed by businesses and by the government.

Corporate debt

The cash needs and financial structure of businesses depend traditionally on the nature of the business: whether it provides products or services; how much investment in plant and equipment is required; the sales cycle and its seasonality. Cash, equity and debt are often referred to as 'corporate finance' and are covered in business courses. The purpose of this section is to give the reader enough information on corporate finance to understand the significance of the use of debt in business finance over time.

Small businesses are often funded by the owner's own investment in the business, which is known as equity. This is the cash flow produced by sales, reinvesting profits and occasionally bank loans. Company growth can similarly be funded by reinvested profits, bank loans and related products (where bankers advance money in exchange for either an interest in or ownership of a portion of the assets). These products can range from leasing a property or series of vehicles, to factoring, where the money owed to a company is collected by a third party who receives a portion of the proceeds collected. All of these techniques are intended to increase the cash available to the company. Larger companies can go to private investors or to the public via the stock exchange to raise new capital, also known as equity, for expansion by giving them a share of the ownership of the company in exchange for cash.

Equity gives the holder rights to a share in the profits and losses of the company, as well as a share in the value of the company should it be sold or closed. Ownership rights also usually come with some say in the decision-making at the company. Debt gives the lender a right to interest on the loan and repayment of the principle amount at maturity. Should the company fail to honour the terms of the contract – full and timely payment of interest and repayment of principle, or other conditions in the loan – the lender may have a right to seize assets or to put the company into bankruptcy.

Traditionally, companies tended to rely on equity for investment, and loans for short-term cash needs – or to fund an acquisition until equity could be raised. Over recent decades, however, two key changes have shifted many companies' search for cash towards debt. The first is an increasing emphasis on both short-term company profits and on increasing returns to shareholders either as dividends paid out of company profits or the increase through the price of their shareholdings. The second is a conscious policy to issue debt instead of equity in the bond markets based on the tax efficiency of corporate debt. The financial cost of debt is considered lower than equity to the extent that the interest on corporate debt is tax deductible for corporate tax purposes in most Western economies, while dividend payments on equity are not tax deductible. Over time many corporations have begun to rely more heavily on debt for funding in order to decrease their overall funding costs. This debt can take the form of traditional bank loans or bonds. Bonds permit investors to subscribe to a company's debt, on which they receive the interest and are repaid principal, taking the credit risk of the company rather than a bank doing so. Bonds can be issued privately or on public markets. They can be bought and sold by investors.[23] After the financial crisis, banks became less willing or able to lend due to their own precarious financial situation, causing an increasing number of companies to turn to public and private debt markets. In addition, low long-term interest rates, resulting from loose central bank monetary policy, made debt a much less expensive source of cash than equity.

The usefulness of debt funding and the appropriate amount of debt for any company depends on many factors. Among the most important are:

— **The stability of the business.** This reflects whether the company produces steady income and profits regardless of the state of the economy. This enables both the company and any lender to understand how much of the company's cash is available to pay interest and repay debt.

— **The company's rate of growth and profitability.** A company that is growing steadily will have an increasing capacity to pay interest and repay debt.

— **The actual level of nominal and real interest rates and their stability.** When real interest rates are negative, i.e. the level of nominal interest minus the rate of inflation is less than zero, it makes economic sense to borrow, as the value of the debt diminishes in real terms with time. However, interest rates can and have changed abruptly, which can affect a company's profitability and ability to continue to pay interest. Dividends on shareholdings are not obligatory, while debt service payments are, so shocks to business models or to the economy that affect a company's revenue or profitability can also reduce the business' ability to pay interest and principal payments on its debt. In a worst case, this can force a company to try and renegotiate its debts or go into bankruptcy.

Chart 4 shows how the volume of financing of debt and equity has changed in percentage terms among UK corporates

"Forgive Us Our Debts"

since 2003. Chart 5 shows the level of UK corporate net debt relative to national GDP, with and without commercial real estate, over a similar period.[24]

Chart 4

Change in Composition of UK Corporate Debt

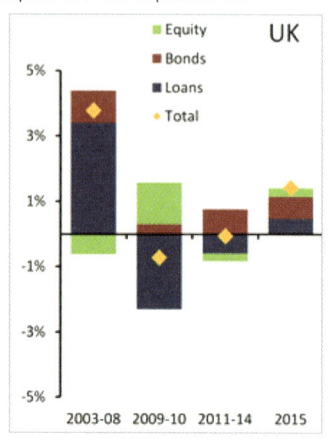

Chart 5

Corporate Debt to Gross Domestic Product in the UK and US

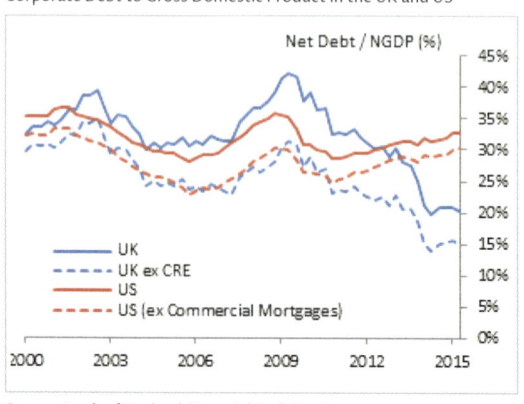

Source: Bank of England Financial Stability Report

Unlike the national debt and personal indebtedness, these charts show that net debt of UK corporates has actually declined dramatically since the financial crisis, and, unlike the US, shows little sign of pick-up. Bonds have largely replaced bank loans. The availability of debt finance suggests that declines are not a function of lack of lending capacity. Rather this speaks to a severe lack of real investment by the private sector in the UK economy. There are several potential reasons for this:

— Low confidence in the future growth of the UK and its major markets.

— Replacement of capital with labour because low wage growth and the growth of the 'gig' economy has made labour cheaper than capital.

— Service industries and the digital economy require less capital than 'old economy' manufacturing, which used plant and equipment.

— A specific UK business climate uncertainty, triggered by the UK's exit from the European Union.

Should we be worried?

Business is far more susceptible to economic, business model or interest rate shocks when debt levels are high. This can have severe societal repercussions, notably in increased unemployment and decreased tax revenues. While current interest rate conditions are unusually low, which might permit increased borrowings, this is offset by two other important considerations. The future uncertainty surrounding Brexit may be making companies cautious about both investment opportunities and their debt levels. There is also considerable change in business conditions happening, notably around technological change and consumer consumption. For example, many retailers are suffering significant competition from internet purchases.

In such circumstances, businesses must choose between financial caution and investment in their future. A misstep can result in a requirement to scale down or even bankruptcy. Both too much debt and too little investment can have secondary effects on economic growth and employment.

However, considering current business model shocks from technology, changing consumer consumption models and the still unknown ramifications of Brexit, there is an argument that now is not the moment for companies to be heavily indebted in spite of a relatively benign interest rate environment.

On the other hand, the lack of investment, due in part to the reasons given above, is a very real concern for long-term economic growth, productivity growth and long-term national wealth. Emphasis on short-term profits can have a major impact on investment, because returns on investments can take some time to work their way through to income, reducing short-term profits. Lack of corporate investment makes the economy increasingly dependent on consumer spending, and diminishes the likelihood of future real wage growth based on productivity growth that permits consumers to repay debt. It appears that corporate shareholders are taking short-term profits at the expense of the consumer.

Public debt

In democracies, we ask governments to provide some services that are difficult or uneconomic to provide individually or privately, for example motorways or national defence. Depending on the choices made by the electorate, voters may decide that government should also provide a broad range of services beyond this, such as employment support, education, healthcare, pensions or disability support. Alternatively, voters may decide that these are not state obligations but rather local government obligations or private decisions. Countries with more private provision of services tend to have lower tax rates. Voters can also choose to use public services and tax as a means of income redistribution, where higher income citizens pay more tax in order to provide services and income support to the unemployed, the retired and the infirm.

Once levels of government intervention are agreed, they need to be funded. The primary vehicle for funding government spending is tax, whether it is collected on an individual's income, from corporations, inheritance or asset or transfer levies or value-added tax (VAT). If governments want to spend more than tax revenue permits, they run a deficit. The shortfall can be made up with borrowing from banks, investors or the general public. In certain circumstances, the central bank can literally print money to fund spending, though such an action in most cases causes an increase of the speed at which prices rise (inflation).

The money raised to fund the deficit is added to the stock of total public debt. Interest must be paid on this debt, and ultimately the principal needs to be repaid or renewed. Interest payments on debt create a circular obligation, as they need to be paid out of tax revenues or borrowed money. Interest rates on government debt will rise and fall in line with both general domestic economic conditions but also upon investors' perception of the willingness and ability of a government to repay the debt.

There are many factors that drive government borrowing. For example the demographic profile of the country will make a difference – i.e. the amount of active working, tax paying citizens versus children or retired people. This can affect both tax revenues and the demand for education, health and retirement support. The overall level of growth in a country will be a key driver of tax revenue, which tends to rise and fall in tandem with growth rates. The third driver is the level and quality of state-provided infrastructure in a country and its need for maintenance and renewal. This can require significant capital spending, though appropriate borrowing for this purpose can be valuable insofar as it tends to raise long-term private sector investment, productivity and growth in an economy.

In addition, during periods of economic difficulty, government can choose to use what is called Keynesian economic policy and stimulate growth and employment through incremental government spending and investment, in the hopes of stimulating economic growth. This can help boost employment and growth, and ultimately tax revenue, to repay the debt incurred in the process if spent well, on infrastructure or education. Spent poorly, it just adds to the deficit and thus the debt that needs to be funded.

Chart 6 below shows the long-term history of UK government borrowing. Prior to the Victorian era, significant borrowing was largely used only to fund wars. Service provision through central government for education only began in 1833 and was not widespread until the end of the 19th century; state retirement provision began only in 1909, and central government funding of healthcare only since 1948. The combination of an increasing role for the state, increasing costs of service provision and a changing demographic profile of the country is leading to significant choices that need to be made between higher tax, lower provision of services and regularly growing government debt.

Chart 6

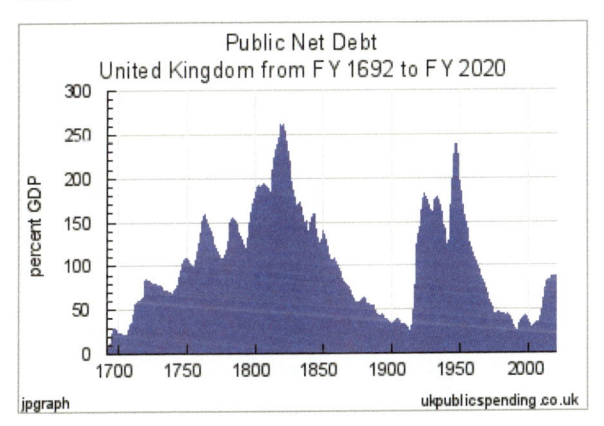

Public Net Debt United Kingdom from FY 1692 to FY 2020

History of UK national debt[25]

In addition, there are arguments that borrowing today is a form of intergenerational inequality, as future generations will have to repay debt incurred to help today's population. This has always been the case, but increasing attention is focused on the subject as the population ages (this results in both a higher cost base from healthcare and state pensions and a lower level of revenue from a lower percentage of the population in active work).

If government deficits are a moral issue due to intergenerational equity, they are also a moral issue as countries determine how the burden of such deficit reduction is shared. For this reason, they need to be considered in light of overall tax and welfare policy and the principle of the 'common good', which refers to the conditions and practices necessary for fostering a shared life in which all are enabled to flourish.

Traditionally, spending reductions fall unequally on those who receive government services and social payments – often the most deprived segments of the population. Tax increases can be structured to disproportionately affect the better off, when only higher rate bands are adjusted upwards, or to increase the burden on the least able to pay, as the short-lived poll tax did in the Thatcher era. Jim Wallis embodied the difficulty of this issue when he wrote: "We must agree not to reduce deficits in ways that further increase poverty and economic inequality by placing the heaviest burdens on those who are already suffering the most.[26]"

If governments choose to reduce their own deficits and debts by reducing welfare payments, and recipients cannot reduce their outgoings proportionately, they will need to borrow. This will effectively transfer public debt into less efficient and more expensive private debt, as the poorest borrowers rely on expensive credit to make ends meet.

Conclusion

This chapter has examined debt in the UK at the personal, business and national level. It has tried to offer a background on the nature of the different kinds of obligations involved, their size, and growth over time. This background will inform, in Chapter 3, a review of the implications of debt with an emphasis on what these contractual obligations do for those who bear them, as well as their relational, societal and intergenerational implications. But first, Chapter 2 provides an overview of Christian teaching on debt and interest and identifies the salient resources for an ethical appraisal of contemporary debt.

1 Hermione Eyre, 'The best of times and the worst of times – in debtors' prison', *The Spectator* 29 October 2016. bit.ly/2EevTh6 (Site accessed: 27/11/2018).

2 Martin Gorsky, 'Self Help and Mutual Aid: Friendly Societies in 19th Century Britain', *Re:FRESH: Recent Findings of Research in Economic and Social History*, 28 (Spring 1999). bit.ly/2EeUlTL (Site accessed: 27/11/2018).

3 'The History of Building Societies', Building Societies Association, 18 April 2017. *bit.ly/2EVgPGF* (Site accessed: 27/11/2018).

4 See the recent IPPR report on *Prosperity and Justice: A Plan for the New Economy*, the final report of the IPPR Commission on Economic Justice, as well as the importance of growth to reduce the importance of national debt on p. 43 of this chapter.

5 Tersa Shano, 'New historical data for assets and liabilities in the UK', *Economic & Labour Market Review* Vol. 2 No. 4. (April 2008). bit.ly/2nLn2gY (Site accessed 27/11/2018).

6 David Prosser, 'Debt: Who is responsible for making sure millions of Britons don't go bust?', *The Independent*, 19 October 2017. *ind.pn/2C88WKO* (Site accessed 27/11/2018).

7 Daniel Harari, 'Household debt: statistics and impact on the economy.' *House of Commons Library*, Briefing Paper No. 7584, 15 December 2017. *researchbriefings.files.parliament.uk/documents/CBP-7584/CBP-7584.pdf* (Site accessed 27/11/2018).

8 Jeremy Black, *Britain Since the Seventies: Politics and Society in the Consumer Age* (London: Reaktion Books Ltd, 2004).

9 Katie Allen, 'Banks cracking down on lending after borrowing binge, survey finds', *The Guardian*, 13 April 2017. bit.ly/2owpFUk (Site accessed 27/11/2018).

10 Troy Segal, 'What is the difference between secured and unsecured debts?', *Investopedia*, updated 29 March 2018, *www.investopedia.com/ask/answers/110614/what-difference-between-secured-and-unsecured-debts.asp* (Site accessed 27/11/2018).

11 *Ibid*.

12 Nominal interest rates are the announced rates, unadjusted for inflation, as distinguished from real interest rates, which are adjusted for the rate of change of prices, or inflation. When real interest rates are below zero, or negative, borrowing is encouraged to stimulate the economy, as debt is essentially cost-free. That is, it is cheaper to borrow than to use cash to pay for goods. A policy of low nominal and real interest rates was used following the global financial crisis to try and stimulate the British economy.

13 See *www.fca.org.uk/firms/consumer-credit-research-debt-management/potential-market-issues* (Site accessed 28/11/2018).

14 Richard Partington, "Rise in personal debt agreements add to concerns about UK debt", *The Guardian*, 27 October 2017, *www.theguardian.com/money/2017/oct/27/rise-in-personal-debt-agreements-add-to-concerns-about-uk-debt* (Site accessed 28/11/2018).

15 The steep pick up since 2004 is due in part to a change in the law that made IVAs much easier to use.

16 Current levels; changes every time.

17 The £100 billion referred to is expressed on prices from 2015, as when this figure was projected, future inflation over the period could not yet be known.

18 Information taken from researchbriefings.parliament.uk/*ResearchBriefing/Summary/SN01079* (Site accessed 28/11/2018).

19 Kevin Peachey, 'Payday loan complaints see sharp rise despite new rules', *BBC News*, 13 June 2017, *www.bbc.co.uk/news/business-40248006* (Site accessed 28/11/2018).

20 *www.fca.org.uk/firms/interest-rate-stress-test* (Site accessed 28/11/2018).

21 Gemma Tetlow, 'How Britons are racking up personal debt', *Financial Times*, 30 June 2017, *www.ft.com/content/61177ca0-5ccf-11e7-b553-e2df1b0c3220*

22 Brian Milligan, BBC News, 29 September 2016, *www.bbc.co.uk/news/business-37504449* (Site accessed 28/11/2018).

23 Institutional investors manage money on behalf of others. For example, they can manage pension funds for corporations, money for charities or group savings of individuals in mutual funds and investment trusts.

24 Christian Schnittker, 'Falling off a cliff: what happened to UK corporate debt? A transatlantic comparison', *Bank Underground*, 22 January 2016, *bankunderground.co.uk/2016/01/22/falling-off-a-cliff-what-happened-to-uk-corporate-debt-a-transatlantic-comparison/* (Site accessed 28/11/2018).

25 *www.ukpublicspending.co.uk/debt_history* (Site accessed 28/11/2018).

26 Wallis, Jim. *The (Un)Common Good: How the gospel brings hope to a world divided.* (Grand Rapids, MI: Brazo Press, 2013), 76.

2
Debt yesterday: debt, interest and usury in Christian thought

Introduction

In this chapter we discuss some of the key features of lending, borrowing, interest and usury in the Bible and the Christian tradition. This is primarily to grasp something of the moral vision of the Christian faith when it comes to debt and debt relations. Encountering morally rich principles may help us think through contemporary debt in the UK and discern ways of making debt relations more humane, fairer and geared towards the common good.

The chapter consists of three main sections: a summary of *biblical theology of debt* that engages with some of the key passages and teaching on lending, borrowing and usury in the Hebrew Bible and New Testament. This is followed by a brief *historical theology of debt*. In this we examine some of the key concerns and teaching of the Church Fathers, in the so-called 'Patristic period', early and late Medieval positions on lending and usury, followed by a foray into the Reformation, homing in on reformers Martin Luther and John Calvin. In the final section we outline three *contemporary theologies of debt*: Jubilee Centre's largely negative appraisals of debt and interest, Kathryn Tanner's 'economy of grace', and Luke Bretherton's reflections on debt's moral ambivalence.

The Christian tradition provides ample resources for thinking through and practically addressing the pressing concerns that arise around personal, corporate and public debt in the UK today. Christianity is an important conversation partner in relation to a discussion of debt because it offers a holistic vision of life and speaks powerfully to the question of the right ordering of economic life and the relationship between lenders and borrowers.

Much of biblical language is economic and financial in nature. This is to be expected. The Christian faith affirms the intrinsic goodness of material life and embodied existence in relationships of reciprocity, mutual care and gift exchange. The very language of Christianity – forgiveness, reckoning, restitution, redemption etc. – is shaped by economic relations and practices.

One of the Bible's overarching narratives concerns liberation from debt slavery. From the book of Exodus to Jesus' ministry on earth, release from debt bondage is a fundamental unifying theme that runs through the entire biblical narrative. Economic language is used to render nothing less than the issue of salvation. As theologian Luke Bretherton puts it, "economic exchanges and debt relations are in fact crucial semantic registers within scriptural and subsequent conceptions of salvation".[1] The language of debt is central in many theological accounts of the significance of Jesus' death (atonement theology). One of the key metaphors for salvation in Christianity is 'redemption', which speaks directly to the idea of a costly release or buy-back from the oppressive grip of sin and guilt. The analogy is between sin and debt,[2] not in the sense that all economic debt is sin or sinful, but in that both can act as oppressive and enslaving forces if they are not covered or eliminated (See Appendix – 'Debt and sin').[3]

The wealth of references and teaching on debt relations within the Christian Scriptures and tradition does not, however, make the task of deriving moral guidance for our contemporary, multi-faith, pluralist context in Britain and our finance-centred and debt-fuelled economy at all easy. If anything, it makes it more difficult. Below we outline some of the biblical teaching on debt relations in the Hebrew Bible and New Testament. The common thread running through these accounts is a concern for human dignity, the flourishing and ability of all to participate in a common life. There is also a strong and particular concern for the welfare of the poor and disenfranchised.

A summary of biblical teaching on debt

We noted earlier that liberation from debt slavery is one of the overarching narratives in the Bible and among the primary templates for salvation. This is clear from the place the book of Exodus has in the biblical canon and its role in framing the biblical story. Genesis ends with the story of Joseph. The Israelites, although saved from famine by Joseph, were reduced to debt servitude alongside Egyptians. They entered into this condition 'voluntarily', but clearly under duress, in exchange for food from Egypt's storehouses, which they themselves had filled up in the first place: "There is nothing left in the sight of my lord but our bodies and our lands...Buy us and our land in exchange for food. We with our land will become slaves to Pharaoh" (Gen. 47:18-19).

In the first part of the book of Exodus a new Pharaoh had come to power and Joseph meant nothing to him (Ex. 1:8). The Pharaoh took advantage of the Israelites' debt slavery and began exploiting them. It is worth pointing out that the Israelites were not chattel slaves or prisoners of war, as is sometimes mistakenly thought, but debt slaves undertaking forced labour.[4] They were freed from this particular condition of debt enslavement. Biblical commentator David Barker observes that the verb *go* in ancient Hebrew is used for both the Exodus and the seventh-year release of debt slaves mentioned in Exodus 21:2 and then taken up in other passages.[5] The connection between the liberation from Egypt and debt slavery is made clear in Leviticus 25:25-43. Given the importance of this passage in discussions of debt and interest in the Bible, it is worth quoting it in full. We will return to some of its specific points later in the chapter:

> *If any of your kin fall into difficulty and become dependent on you, you shall support them; they shall live with you as though resident aliens. Do not take interest in advance or otherwise make a profit from them, but fear your God; let them live with you. You shall not lend them your money at interest taken in advance, or provide them food at a profit. I am the Lord your God, who brought you out of the land of Egypt, to give you the land of Canaan, to be your God.*
>
> *If any who are dependent on you become so impoverished that they sell themselves to you, you shall not make them serve as slaves. They shall remain with you as hired or bound labourers. They shall serve with you until the year of the jubilee. [See Appendix, 'Did the Jubilee ever happen?']. Then they and their children with them shall be free from your authority; they shall go back to their own family and return to their ancestral property. For they are my servants, whom I brought out of the land of Egypt; they shall not be sold as slaves are sold. You shall not rule over them with harshness, but shall fear your God.*[6]

The prescriptions clearly seek inclusion of all in a common life ("let them live with you"). Interest-free loans are to be made to the poor as a form of gift, in recognition of the fact that both lender and borrower belong to the same body politic – in Israel's case, as 'people of the covenant'. The prohibition of usury and the limits placed on debt slavery, leading up to the institution of the Jubilee, are grounded in God's act of liberating his covenanted people from debt bondage in Egypt.

Exodus, with its central drama of liberation, is one of the key templates for Jesus' life, death and resurrection. The New

Testament presents Jesus' mission and the accomplishment of his death as 'redemption' from debt to sin (Mk. 10:45; Rom. 6:21-23; Col. 3:5-6). The Jubilee frames Jesus' own announcement of his mission. At the beginning of his ministry, Jesus appropriated the words of the prophet Isaiah, saying:

> *The Spirit of the Lord is upon me, because he has anointed me to proclaim good news to the poor. He has sent me to proclaim release for the captives and recovery of sight for the blind, to let the oppressed go free, to proclaim the year of the Lord's favour.*

The text continues:

> *He rolled up the scroll, gave it back to the attendant, and sat down. The eyes of all in the synagogue were fixed on him. Then he began to say to them, 'Today this scripture has been fulfilled in your hearing' (Luke 4:18-21).*

The community of Christ followers that emerged at the end of Jesus' ministry, as recounted in Acts 2, was "a Jubilee community where no one has debts"[7] because "all who believed were together and had all things in common; they would sell their possessions and goods and distribute the proceeds to all, as any had need" (Acts 2:44-45).

In the biblical vision, all use of money is tied to a person's salvation. Money is a powerful force that can enslave us to our self-interested desires. To pursue money at the expense of people's welfare and the common good is nothing short of opposing God and forfeiting salvation. Jesus presented a stark choice: "You cannot serve both God and wealth" (Matt. 6:24). A key mark of salvation is how we relate to those around us, particularly the poor and vulnerable. This includes, but is not limited to, the financial resources at our disposal. Those who use resources selfishly, instead of giving and lending to those in need, are not merely wrong or foolish, but stand condemned. As we will see, the Medieval theologians and canonists picked up on this radical teaching and explained what is at stake in the misuse of resources and mistreatment of the needy.

The broader context for teaching on debt in the Bible is the right ordering of economic life in line with the responsibility to steward, that is, justly care for and administer creation (Gen. 1.26-28),[8] and to love God and neighbour. According to Jesus' answer in Matthew 22:40 this was the summation of the Law and Prophets. Specific teaching on debt in the Bible is intimately connected to the issue of the function and proper use of the land by the people of God. In the Old Testament, land was not simply a resource to be disposed of at will, but a gift, an integral part of the fulfilment of God's promise to Abraham, and therefore the basis of Israel's unique identity as a covenanted people. The next section unpacks the biblical vision of land and people.

Land and people in the Bible

Neither land nor people are resources to be employed in purely self-interested economic pursuits. Such commodification is foreign to the biblical vision. Made for relationship with God and bearing God's image, people have inherent dignity and worth. The land and its resources are a gift for the flourishing of all.

In biblical times, ownership was a relational rather than an absolute good. You owned land to produce and thereby participate in the common life of the community to which you belonged. This relational understanding of property sits in tension with centuries of practice of individual property law in most countries. Only God is recognised in the biblical vision as the owner of land. People, whether residents or sojourners, are only stewarding tenants called to develop relationships of mutual responsibility and care, forging a common life where all can flourish.[9]

Throughout the scriptures, God displays a particular concern for the poor, the overlooked and the voiceless at the margins of society, away from the centre of political, social and economic power. The various laws in Exodus, Leviticus and Deuteronomy concerning the freeing of slaves and the use of land that regulate Israel's economic life were intended as checks against the commodification of people and land. Indeed, the Old Testament Law never sanctions the trading of slaves, let alone condones a market in slavery.[10] The Law allowed, however, people unable to repay debts to sell themselves into slavery (more accurately, debt servitude). This was tightly regulated as a temporary arrangement. In the same way, it allowed Israelite lenders to 'buy' such debt slaves. They would remain in servitude in order to repay their debts for no more than six years and would be released in the seventh year (Ex. 21:1-6).[11]

The biblical vision therefore prioritises the welfare of people, understood to be embedded in a nexus of relationships, and the health of the land over personal gain and profit (Ex. 23:10-11).[12] The land was the fundamental means of subsistence and the basis of citizenship. Out of concern for people, strict regulation was in place to prevent permanent expropriation of land and to maintain the integrity of the community bound up by the covenant between God and the people of Israel. At the heart of the Jubilee legislation (Lev. 25:1-4, 8-10) was the aim of controlling the disparity between the rich and the poor and preventing misfortunes and adverse economic circumstances to be exploited for selfish gain by others. Selling land in perpetuity and enslaving those who were part of the covenantal community or 'fellowship' was seen "as simultaneously undermining the political order and the character and identity of the people."[13]

The extensive Old Testament regulation was aimed at sustaining a shared life where all were enabled to flourish, as opposed to a situation where some prospered at the expense of others. Justice, understood as right relationships among people and between people and the wider environment, was central to Old Testament legislation and biblical teaching as a whole. The welfare of the poor, the economically, socially and culturally marginalised was the main concern behind the legislation around lending.

Lending and borrowing

It is against this backdrop that we must understand the specific regulation concerning lending and borrowing. In Old Testament times, and subsistence economies more generally, people would be forced to borrow in cases of crops failing or animal sickness, among other extreme circumstances. Lending – without interest – and borrowing were permitted as means of both expressing and cultivating relationships of reciprocity and interdependence within the community (Deut. 15:8). Lending freely to those in need was a clear mark of righteousness or right relatedness (Ps. 15:5), a mechanism for restoring equality and ensuring inclusion in the community.

When lending occurred, the Torah placed strict restrictions on the collateral that might be taken: that is, the asset that the borrower lost to the creditor in case of default or failure to keep up with payments. This was to prevent a loan from destroying the livelihood of the borrower. Exodus 22:26-38 notes:

If you take your neighbour's cloak in pawn, you shall restore it before the sun goes down; for it may be your neighbour's only clothing to use as cover; in what else shall that person sleep? And if your neighbour cries out to me, I will listen, for I am compassionate.

Charging interest or practicing usury,[14] however, was strictly prohibited within the community of Israel. Exodus 22:25 notes: "If you lend money to my people, to the poor among you, you shall not deal with them as a creditor; you shall not exact interest from them." In a subsistence economy, exacting interest was a sure means of driving one's neighbour further into poverty. This made interest a tool wielded by the economically powerful to oppress and exploit the misfortunes and vulnerabilities of the poor. Underlying the ban was the sense that poor and rich alike belong to the same body politic, embedded within relations of trust, mutual responsibilities and obligations, and with equal dignity as made in the image of God.

The book of Nehemiah, charting the story of Israel centuries later as its leaders returned from exile in Babylon, paints a picture of abuse and exploitation within the community. Less well-off Israelites were forced to go into debt slavery to secure food from the rich or to pay their taxes to the king. The community leader Nehemiah was incensed and called the 'nobles and officials' to repentance. He asked specifically that they stop charging interest and pay back what they had taken through extortion (Neh. 5:10-11).

The prophets were particularly critical against structural injustice; arrangements designed to systematically disadvantage the poor. Prophetic literature is filled with critical references to "dishonest scales", double measures and other devices used to exploit and disadvantage the less well off. Jeremiah railed against those who set up snares to catch people (Jer. 5:26-28). Amos denounced the abusive practices of usurers that sold the basic possessions of the poor, even the poor themselves, when they could not pay their debts: "They sell the righteous for silver, and the needy for a pair of sandals" (Amos 2:6). Micah similarly castigated lenders who seized the fields and houses of those in their debt (Mic. 2:1-2).

But there was no universal ban on interest. Charging interest to foreigners, who were outside of, and unknown within, the covenant community, was permitted. At first sight, this seems like a dubious double standard. Indeed, this has baffled many biblical commentators through the centuries. Examined closely, however, permission of interest in loans to foreigners reveals a realistic concern for maintaining the integrity of a common life by mitigating against the resultant risks of default, deliberate or otherwise. It also levelled the playing field with neighbouring nations, which practiced interest in commercial transactions. (Deut.15:3, 23:20; Lev. 25:39-54). John Calvin helpfully explained the rationale for this practice. He wrote:

> *Looking at the political law, no wonder God permitted his people to exact fenory [excessive charging of interest] from foreigners: because otherwise mutual reciprocity would not have obtained, without which one side must needs be injured. God commands his people not to practise fenory, and therefore by this law lays the obligation on the Jews alone, not on foreign peoples. Therefore, in order that analogous conditions may prevail, he concedes the same liberty to his people that the Gentiles were arrogating to themselves, because precisely this moderation is tolerable, where the position of both parties is the same and equal.*[15]

This is a particularly perceptive commentary that gets at the issue of power dynamics in lending and borrowing and shows the concern for sharing risk. Calvin sees that relationships of mutuality between members of the same covenant community cannot be expected to obtain outside of it.

New Testament scholar Klyne R. Snodgrass shows that the discussion of interest in ancient Palestine was complicated and it is likely that no prohibition on business loans was in effect in the 1st century.[16]

The Lord's prayer: "forgive us our debts"

The Lord's prayer, as it has come to be known, appears twice in the gospels, in Matthew 6 and Luke 11. The more complete version in Matthew gives the title of this report: "And forgive us our debts, as we also have forgiven our debtors."[17] The plea intriguingly marries the spiritual with the material and economic. The first debt mentioned in the plural is spiritual in nature – we do not in fact have economic debts to God. Debt is an analogy for sin, which attracts judgement and leads to loss of authentic freedom.[18] The latter debt is economic in nature and takes place within horizontal relations. Biblical commentator R. T. France notes that the term used is the Aramaic word for sin, which clearly indicates a financial debt. The point is that we cannot request, let alone expect, forgiveness from God while withholding it from others economically 'indebted to us', as Luke puts it.

> **The cancellation of debts was meant to ensure that all members of society had access to productive assets and participated meaningfully in the common life.**

Here we have at the very least the basis of both an individual and social ethics of forgiveness of economic debt.

Forgiveness of economic debt reflects the forgiveness of sin, which we have seen is one of the key features of salvation. This is consonant with the principle that debt forgiveness is not only fitting but also sometimes necessary. The Year of Jubilee mentioned in Leviticus 25, which the Lord's prayer echoes, entailed the cancellation of all debts and the return of the land to its original owners. This was meant to ensure that all members of society had access to productive assets and participated meaningfully in the common life. Jesus' injunction powerfully echoed this Jubilee tradition, which prescribed wholesale debt cancellation.

Deriving an ethics of debt from these passages that goes beyond the personal to the business or national levels is, however, a difficult task, on account of the absence of such structures in those times and the broader economic, political and cultural differences between 1st-century Palestine and contemporary life in the UK. As Anderson rightly points out, "in the contemporary economy...most debt is commercial and it is taken on by economic agents who are able to use their human capital to generate income from which to repay the debt. Any requirement that banks or other institutions making such loans must forgive debt ultimately hurts both the poor and the non-poor."[19] Chapter 3 explores how the concept of debt forgiveness as found in the Lord's prayer has been implemented, in spirit more so than in letter, and how we can continue to see modern incarnations of it today, notwithstanding the differences between the economic system of ancient Palestine and the economic system of today.

Lend expecting nothing in return?

The Lord's prayer is not the only place where Jesus discussed lending in striking terms. In Luke 6:35 Jesus radicalised Old Testament teaching on lending without interest: "Lend, expecting nothing in return." While the Old Testament encouraged lending freely, especially to those in need, Jesus encouraged his followers to treat loans as gifts and to be prepared never to recover their assets. It could be argued that Jesus was calling for lenders to share the risks associated with the loans they were giving out. Intriguingly, Jesus addressed lenders rather than borrowers. Then, as now, lenders had more cultural power than borrowers, even as they clearly depended on the latter.

In Matthew 5:42 Jesus amplified the commandment, noting: "Give to everyone who begs from you, and do not refuse anyone who wants to borrow from you." This is arguably not a call to indiscriminate lending, but to differentiated lending. Faithful to the Torah's particular concern for the poor, Jesus laid down a particular ethical regime for lending to the one "who begs from you", the poor, and to do so with generosity and open-handedness. By implication, this created a different ethical regime for lending where there is a greater symmetry between creditor and debtor. Through these injunctions, Jesus was encouraging lenders to know their borrowers, understand their true situation, needs and vulnerabilities. Elsewhere he further radicalised the teaching on lending, asking his disciples, "If you lend to those from whom you expect repayment, what credit is that to you? Even sinners lend to sinners, to receive as much again. But love your enemies, do good, and lend, expecting nothing in return" (Luke 6:34-35). Jesus commanded not only risky lending within the community, but, strikingly, to those outside it, to "enemies". He broadened the boundaries in which lending should be practiced as a means of love and practical assistance in time of need.

Talents and minas: what might parables have to do with debt?

"Obligation/debt is a major theme in Jesus' parables", says New Testament scholar Klyne R. Snodgrass in his book *Stories with Intent: A Comprehensive Guide to the Parables of Jesus.*[20] Jesus' parables are famously and frustratingly both simple and ambivalent in their meaning.[21] There is no shortage of attempts to either restrict their range of meaning – what point or points they are making[22] – and hence their contemporary applications, or to show a plethora of possible meanings and choose the one that best aligns with, and supports, the readers' already established views and commitments. We dare not pretend, therefore, that we ourselves are entirely objective and free from all bias.

Apart from their primary spiritual meaning and applications, having to do with the Gospel of the Kingdom and how disciples are to 'put it to work' in the world until Jesus' return, both the parable of the talents, and the parable of the minas, in Matthew 25 and Luke 19 respectively, support not just commercial enterprise and entrepreneurial savviness – this is clear –[23] but also the emphasis on productive investment. The worst thing to do, in the order of priority, is to leave money fallow and not use it productively. Lending at interest gives a small return but is not nearly as valuable as investing it productively in something that creates more than existed before.

Neither the parable of the talents nor the parable of the minas says that charging or gaining interest on loans is disallowed and immoral. In both of the parables, the third servant, who only returns the original amount given for investment purposes, is reprimanded for not investing the money with bankers so that "on my return I would have received what was my own with interest". Emphatically, however, this text does not in itself legitimate or discredit any particular economic and financial system or theory (e.g. modern banking and interest-based finance), let alone suggest God is a "rapacious capitalist".[24] Chapter 3 shows how the varied wisdom of the Christian Scriptures and tradition of reflection on debt can be fruitfully brought to bear on the contemporary economic context in the UK.

Historical theology of debt: a brief overview

The Patristic period

The prohibition on charging interest on loans – or usury as it was originally known (before it came to mean extortionate and often illegal levels of interest) – was maintained throughout Christian history up to the modern period. It was a key concern of the Church councils. The Council of Nicea (325 AD) directly condemned usury practised by clergy. The ban was upheld and extended to the laity at the Council of Clichy (626 AD), and became incorporated into Canon Law from about 1140 onward. In the UK, usury laws were repealed as late as 1854.

Christian theologians during the Patristic period (100-450 AD) condemned interest as incompatible with Christian love, viewing money and property as a means to contribute to the common good rather than for selfish pursuits and personal gain. Although civil law permitted interest, John Chrysostom called believers to go beyond what the law permitted and to act according to the manner of love established by Christ. In the 4th century, Basil the Great, Bishop of Caesarea in Cappadocia (now modern Turkey) unequivocally condemned lending at interest. In one of his writings he remarked that a loan given on interest is a poison that slowly destroys the life of the borrower.[25] Usury, he noted, creates a perverse reversal of charity, by which the poor pay more, while capital-rich lenders amass more wealth. The poor end up giving to the rich, rather than the other way around. The strong words against lending at interest come from a belief that the cardinal commandment for the Christian is love of neighbour. Hoarding and holding on to possessions when your neighbour is in dire need is a lamentable failure to love. This view rests on a view of resources and goods as gifts that should be kept in circulation rather than amassed – a far cry from the modern view of absolute property rights. Describing Basil's economic vision, Bishop Graham Tomlin notes: "The circulation of capital, and the rejection of the practice of hoarding of goods or money, is all in the service of what he calls *epanisoun* – a restoration of balance or equilibrium within society so that all can flourish."[26]

Far from being a minority report, the ban on interest was shared by virtually every Christian writer of the era. It was a principled stance against lending money as a means of preying on the poor and exploiting their misfortune for swift profit. The Church Fathers consistently enjoined Christians to meet and respond to the poor as Christ had responded to their spiritual poverty – with generosity and love, not as an opportunity for profit.

The Medieval period

The Medieval theologians and canonists followed a similar line of thinking, upholding the ban on usury and arguing strongly against any form of unlawful profit. A culturally forbidden practice for many centuries, usury was formally banned and condemned by the Third Lateran Council in 1179 and then at the Second Council of Lyons in 1274,

Christian scholars and theologians working between the 13th and 15th centuries (also known as the 'scholastics') equated usury with robbery, explaining it as a clear violation of the seventh commandment in the Ten Commandments (Ex. 20).[27] As such, it was considered a mortal sin. Dante famously placed usurers in the third ring of hell (*Inferno*, canto 17). Time, the scholastics argued, was a universal good for all to enjoy, rather than a means of profit through the charging of interest. Not only a breaking of a divine command, the scholastics also viewed usury as unnatural, going against the true use of money which, as they saw it, was to facilitate exchange. Money, they argued, is sterile and should not be pursued as an end in itself.

The Medieval prohibition of usury was part of a more expansive vision for life in which people participated in sharing both material and spiritual goods, the abundance of the created world, out of mutual love and with justice in distributing the goods for the sustenance of all. Usury, in this vision, was the refusal to share and thus meet the basic needs of the borrower: "Usurious lending compounds the injustice of keeping from the needy neighbour what is rightfully his – namely, one's superfluities, and even more, it compounds the uncharitableness of not sacrificing of one's necessaries to relieve his distress."[28]

But Medieval theologians also began to distinguish usury from legitimate interest. This was in a context where feudalism was giving way to an economy shaped around urban financial centres, wealthy patrons such as the Medici family, redefined functions of the state, expansion of the Church and new opportunities for trade. They offered wide-ranging and detailed discussions about the different types of loans and the instances where interest may be duly charged. For example, as a kind of insurance against loss to compensate the lender for the risk taken in offering credit, for loan processing and managing fees (remuneration) and indemnity fees (when payment would be delayed). Interest also began to be permissible when it was established that the lender could make a higher profit by using the money for some other productive endeavour. Interest was, in those cases, considered a form of recompense (*lucrum cessans*). In modern economic parlance this is known as the opportunity cost. These innovations were crucial in distinguishing lending for subsistence from lending for starting or developing a business, but also from lending for financial profit alone. Through these distinctions the Church was creating opportunities, albeit limited ones, for investment and credit that would be used for the welfare of the poor and the vulnerable, who could not provide for themselves either through work or whose very livelihood depended on a loan.[29] The end or final purpose of borrowing and lending became decisive factors in ethical evaluations of interest.

However, the growing distinctions and concessions that were made never did away with the principle that economic relations were subordinate to, and embedded within, social relations. Profit was allowed so long as risk was shared between parties. One of the central concerns was that money and profit did not crowd out other considerations – moral and relational – in crafting a common life.

The Reformation

The story is often told that the Reformers relaxed the teaching on usury and paved the way for modern capitalism. That is only half-true. The Reformation did not change very much in the scholastic view of usury. Urlich Zwingli, Martin Luther, Philip Melanchton and John Calvin condemned excessive usury with one voice. But, rather than taking a disciplinary approach appealing to and reinforcing rules

– they responded to the social dangers of usury primarily by attempting "to create an ethics of virtue in society in which charity was to train the freed conscience to recognize and resist usury".[30]

The Reformers built on the by then clear distinction between commercial loans, which were used for investment and profit between equal parties and on agreed terms, and loans made to the poor in times of hardship and contracted under duress. Merchant capitalism slowly emerged from Medieval feudal forms of social and economic activity. Lending and borrowing at interest drove entrepreneurial activity and enabled access to capital for the economically disadvantaged. Profits began to be shared between borrowers and lenders. Interest/usury became a means of economic development and wealth growth.

It should therefore be unsurprising that attitudes to lending began to shift.

Martin Luther radicalised the teaching on usury for Christian borrowers and lenders alike. The basis for his uncompromising ethics for lending and other commercial practices was nothing short than Christ's call to perfection or, in a different translation, completeness, wholeness or wholeheartedness (Matt. 5:48). He instructed Christian borrowers whose property has been seized unjustly to acquiesce without resistance.[31] The morally right thing to do, he argued, was to eschew revenge and simply give up your

> "The Reformers built on the by then clear distinction between commercial loans, which were used for investment and profit between equal parties and on agreed terms, and loans made to the poor in times of hardship and contracted under duress.

possessions. But he had equally radical instruction for lenders. He was adamantly against charging interest. In his view, to charge interest on a loan violated three fundamental laws: the law of Christ, according to which lending is to be a gratuitous act, the law of natural equity, according to which profit should not be sought at the loss of your neighbour, and the law of love, which requires loving your neighbours as yourself. Lending was permitted, he argued, only if done freely and out of love for neighbours in need.

Luther showed no particular enthusiasm for the commercial sphere of exchange. Activity in this area was merely permitted, not commanded by God, Luther argued. Still, even in this sphere Luther focused on risk and continued to uphold the traditional emphases on equity in exchange and 'just price'. In his view, we have a God-given relation to temporal goods that is inevitably marked by risk. To devise strategies for overcoming risk at all costs displayed avarice, which in turn corrupted the dynamic of exchange and the participants in the exchange. He condemned "all practices that enable the merchant to 'make safe, certain and continual profit out of unsafe, uncertain, and perishable goods.'"[32] All practices that shielded the lender against the risks associated with normal economic exchange were off limit. The lender should share risks – and losses – with the borrower whenever these occur.

John Calvin also remained sensitive to the potential for abuse towards the poor in lending and borrowing. Yet he refused to condemn lending at interest altogether, pointing out that Scripture nowhere unequivocally forbids it wholesale: "If we totally prohibit the practice of usury", he wrote, "we would restrain consciences more rigidly than God himself."[33] He was, however, acutely aware of the dangers that come with usury (or interest) and advised real caution: "If we permit it, then some under this guise would be content to act with unbridled licence, unable to abide any limits." Usury, he wrote, has two companions which follow it closely behind: radical cruelty and the art of deception. In the end, he asserted, "it would be desirable if usurers were chased from every country, even if the practice were unknown",[34] echoing something of Luther's biting rhetoric.

He realised, however, that the times had changed. A total prohibition had become impossible. If it was there to stay, usury or lending at interest should "at least [be used] for the common good", he wrote. Calvin went on to outline a series of safeguards for keeping debt aligned with the common good. First, he instructed that interest on loans to the poor should be forbidden. This of course entails that the lender seeks to understand the financial situation of the borrower. Second, borrowing and lending should be practiced according to the principle of equity: "do unto others as you would have them to do unto you". Finally, attention should be given not merely to the private interests of the individual borrowers and lenders, but, as Calvin put it, "we should keep in mind what is best for the common good".[35] This ethical imperative does not straightforwardly translate into an economic policy, but offers a fruitful ethical framework for assessing debt relations.

Contemporary theologies of debt

As we have seen there are a number of historical Christian positions on the question of debt. This remains the case today. Below we outline three that we believe are most pertinent to the conversation this report seeks to stimulate on debt's moral underpinnings and relational consequences.

Jubilee Centre

The researchers and practitioners affiliated with the Jubilee Centre, a Christian think tank based in Cambridge UK, articulate what can be described as a radical position. They take a largely negative view of debt, its normalisation in the modern economic environment and debt-finance more broadly.[36] This is based largely on close readings of, and extrapolations from individual biblical texts, mostly from the Old Testament, on lending and borrowing.[37] The approach also rests on the theological premise that the teaching of the Torah is universally relevant and applicable, with appropriate adaptation, to contemporary society.

There is a strong focus on individual responsibility but there are broader criticisms against centralised political authority, the modern financial system dependent on central and large commercial banks ('loaning money into existence'), inflation, seen as an unjust means of reducing a government's debt obligations, and other features of the modern economic system.[38] In *Crumbling Foundations: a biblical critique of modern money*, Guy Brandon suggests the need to develop 'positive money' that is not 'created hand-in-hand with debt', as is the case with the modern monetary system, which is deemed to be inherently unjust.[39]

Indebtedness is presented as form of slavery, "because of the solemn promise to repay",[40] and corrosive to relationships.[41] Always and everywhere, interest is "reaping where you did not sow" (Matt. 25:24), and therefore immoral.[42] There is little attempt made to distinguish between different kinds of indebtedness in the contemporary context, for example between a mortgage and a payday loan with very high interest rates. There is therefore no attempt to offer a differentiated ethical evaluation of contemporary debt relations. To take on debt is to presume on a fundamentally unknown future, an arrogance deemed to negatively impact individual wellbeing and human social relations. Debt also restricts freedom and the flexibility required of Christian disciples to follow the lead of God. Economic debt is contrasted with equity-based finance and found wanting by comparison. While motivated primarily by theological convictions, Jubilee Centre economist Paul Mills puts forward a pragmatic case against debt-finance and argues in favour of equity contracts that, at least in theory, share risks and rewards.[43]

Kathryn Tanner

In her writings, particularly in the *Economy of Grace*,[44] theologian Kathryn Tanner seeks to do more than simply inject a moral ethos into the economy. She shows how the Christian story has its own alternative economic vision for the production, exchange and circulation of goods. Its beating heart is grace – the Triune God in perpetual self-giving action. Grace is the basis and the driver of an economic vision built around unconditional and universal giving,[45] and "non-competitive" economic relations,[46] where "goods circulate...for the benefit of others".[47]

A truly Christian economy, according to Tanner, is one of grace and gift. God, she argues, is fundamentally a gift giver not a lender – the giver of all gifts and the supreme gift of his Son, who cancels all debts to sin. The story of the Bible is one in which God continually, persistently, even relentlessly, seeks to communicate his generosity with the world. Creation, covenant, redemption, consummation in Christ are all, according to Tanner, modes of divine giving or what she calls 'giftfulness'.[49] Unconditional giving is the defining feature of the 'economy of grace' that covers "both God's relations to us, in their diversity, and our relations with each other".[50] Because

God is by definition an unconditional gift giver he cannot be repaid in principle. This does not mean, however, that humans therefore owe an infinite, unpayable debt to God. This is where negotiating the right relationship between atonement theology and theological ethics of economics is vitally important. In Tanner's view, the death of Jesus is not the payment or clearing of the debt humanity supposedly owes to God, rather it is the dismantling of the debt system and the salvation from the consequences of the debt economy.[51] The cross is the true and ultimate Jubilee to which the Jubilee years prescribed in the Old Testament had been pointing to: an action by which debts are forgiven rather than paid, debt slaves are freed rather than temporarily eased of their burden.

Whatever the application of this vision for the broader society in the contemporary context might look like, the applications for the Church are clear. The Church is called to reflect the gift-giving God it worships and practice 'giftfulness'. It does this not to pay back debts to God, but as a way of expressing Christian identity: persons in relationship living under grace. By reflecting God's 'giftfulness' in all human relations, the Church lives the "only way of life appropriate to the way things are" in light of the Christian Gospel.[52] Indeed, Christians are already taking a leading role in church-based credit unions and holistic debt counselling, countering the problem of rising and often crippling personal debt. Such initiatives can easily be taken as applications of the principle of 'giftfulness'. There is, however, ample room for developing imaginative initiatives to resist excessive consumption and practice responsible stewardship and entrepreneurship.

Luke Bretherton

Theologian Luke Bretherton of Duke University notes the difficulty of speaking about debt. Debt, he shows, is a complex phenomenon that exists simultaneously on two axes. The first of these has, at one end, ontological debt or obligations inherent in the fact of existence – the debt owed to God, nature, country, ancestors etc. – and, at the other, economic debt. The second axis on which debt circulates is the axis of mutuality and domination. Just as debt can be simultaneously ontological and economical, it can express and facilitate relations of mutuality but also be a means of domination and coercion. This deep ambivalence makes debt a perplexing phenomenon.

In Bretherton's view, economic debt is not inherently immoral or problematic. At its best, he argues, lending and borrowing are practices that express and encourage relationships of reciprocity and gift exchange, which "entail[s] a tangled interplay of freedom and obligation".[53] This view is underpinned by a relational anthropology, the view that we are constituted as human beings by our relationships – to God, to nature and to one another – and flourish in relationships of mutual obligations (debts) and gift exchange. Bretherton refuses to see debt and gift in opposition and does not separate debt from obligation.

Rather than dismissed wholesale, Bretherton believes debt should be assessed on the purpose for which it is incurred, the ends to which it is orientated and the quality of relationships it establishes between persons, institutions and the physical world. Where these are relationships of reciprocity and responsible stewardship towards the environment, debt is legitimate. Problems arise when debt relations are disembedded from the realm of human social relations, and moral considerations are bracketed out. When debt fundamentally alters the relationship between lender and borrower and puts the borrower at net disadvantage, legislative checks and regulatory protections, such as interest rates capping, are needed to protect the more vulnerable parties in the exchange. This is to prevent indebtedness turning into debt bondage, "thereby dissolving the conditions for equitable relations between members of the same body politic."[54] If the goal is to foster and maintain a common life, where all are able to participate in a shared space for meaning and action, certain measures are necessary to preserve equitable relations and prevent domination.

In the contemporary context, still dominated by a contractual view of social relations, "good citizenship and political order are not seen to be threatened by usurious forms of personal and national debt."[55] Because the defining feature of the modern subject of the social contract is freedom of choice, the concern to place limits and ensure debt relations are a means of cultivating reciprocity rather than exploitation wanes from public attention (see Appendix – 'Free to borrow?'). It is assumed borrowers are freely choosing individuals who have full knowledge of the contracts they enter and who should therefore bear the consequences of their actions. Jeremy Bentham's views from the 1780s about the irrationality and pointlessness of anti-usury measures still hold sway in the public imagination.[56] This is most clearly seen in the current finance-dominated capitalism, where "debt is divorced from mutuality and used to subjugate, command, manage, order, and normalize particular behaviours."[57] Debt is normalised. This gives rise to "regimes of indebtedness [which] create[s] dependency and vulnerability and concentrates power in the hands of those who control the means of credit." Housing, healthcare, education and other essential "social means of citizenship" become determined by debt.[58]

Normalised economically, debt comes to dominate subjectively, "by inducing feelings of shame, guilt, and inferiority: to be moral, righteous, and just is to be responsible and pay back what you owe."[59] This is much more difficult advice to follow when a person is "increasingly burdened with an infinite series of debts, whether at the personal level (payday lenders, mortgages, and the like) or in our public life (sovereign debt), then we are constantly made to feel morally suspect. Our credit score becomes a placeholder for our character."[60]

Against the expansion of dominating, exploitative debt relations and "the faux morality of finance capitalism," the Christian story, he writes, speaks powerfully "about a God who comes to a people in debt bondage and makes a way where there is no way, who lavishes credit on those the world considers subprime, who riskily invests, to the point of emptying himself, in those who cannot repay, and who seeks a dividend of love and Sabbath fruitfulness, not of material prosperity."

1 Luke Bretherton, *Christ and the Common Life: A Guide to Political Theology* (Grand Rapids, MI: Eerdmans, 2019). At the time of publication, Prof Bretherton's new book had not been released, hence the absence of a page number. In this report, all quotations from this book are taken from an advanced draft which the author kindly made available to us.

2 In the Bible sin refers not simply to misdeeds and individual wrongdoing, but to a cosmic, corrupting and "malevolent agency bent upon despoiling, imprisonment, and death – the utter undoing of God's purposes." See Fleming Rutledge, *Crucifixion: Understanding the Death of Jesus Christ* (Grand Rapids, MI: Eerdmans, 2015), p. 175. For a more detailed discussion of the relation between debt and sin, see Appendix, 'Debt and sin'.

3 E. Philip Davies, *The Crisis and the Kingdom: Economics, Scripture, and the Global Financial Crisis* (Eugene, OR: Cascade, 2012), p. 70.

4 Luke Bretherton, 'Neither a Borrower Nor a Lender Be?' in *God and the Moneylenders: Faith and the Battle against Exploitative Lending* eds. Angus Ritchie & David Barclay, The Centre for Theology & Community (London: The Centre for Theology & Community, 2013), p. 32.

5 David Barker, *Tight Fists or Open Hands? Wealth and Poverty in Old Testament Law* (Grand Rapids, MI: Eerdmans, 2009), p. 140.

6 Leviticus 25:25-43.

7 Luke Bretherton, *Resurrecting Democracy: Faith, Citizenship, and the Politics of a Common Life* (Cambridge: Cambridge University Press, 2015), p. 246.

8 The term 'environment' is foreign to the biblical imaginary. The anthropocentrism of the term 'environment' is at odds with the biblical vision in which humanity exists in a state of close interdependence and has a clear responsibility of care and stewardship towards the non-human creation – animal and physical alike.

9 Luke Bretherton, *Resurrecting Democracy: Faith, Citizenship, and the Politics of a Common Life* (Cambridge: Cambridge University Press, 2015), p. 247

10 Andy Hartropp, 'Socioeconomic justice in the Old Testament: What is it?' in *Journal of the Association of Christian Economists*, No. 22 (December, 1996), p. 4.

11 Although after the six years, slaves could choose to remain in the household of their masters as hired servants if they wished.

12 Ex. 23:10-11: "For six years you shall sow your land and gather in its yield; but the seventh year you shall let it rest and lie fallow, so that the poor of your people may eat; and what they leave the wild animals may eat. You shall do the same with your vineyard, and with your olive orchard."

13 Luke Bretherton, *Resurrecting Democracy: Faith, Citizenship, and the Politics of a Common Life* (Cambridge: Cambridge University Press, 2015), p. 248.

14 For much of Christian history interest and usury are interchangeable. It is only much later that usury came to refer to extortionate levels of interest.

15 From Calvin's 1575 letter to Claude de Sachin. Quoted from translation by André Biéler, *Calvin's Economic and Social Thought*, trans., James Greig (Geneva: WCC Publications, 2005), p. 404.

16 Klyne R. Snodgrass, Stories with Intent: *A Comprehensive Guide to the Parables of Jesus* (Grand Rapids, MI: Eerdmans, 2008), Kindle edition. Location 1551/0/2572.

17 Matthew 6:12.

18 See Appendix for a brief discussion of the relationships between 'Debt and sin'.

19 John E. Anderson, 'Government Debt and Deficits', *Faith & Economics*, 61/62, (Spring/Fall 2013), p. 7.

20 Klyne R. Snodgrass, *Stories With Intent: A Comprehensive Guide to the Parables of Jesus* (Grand Rapids, MI: Eerdmans, 2008), Kindle edition: location 1545.0/2572. He writes: "In addition to these two parables [The Talents and the Minas – Matt 25:14-30; Luke 19:11-27] compare the parables of the Unforgiving Servant (Matt 18:23-25), the Two Sons (Matt 21-28-32), the Wicked Tenants (Matt 21:33-45/Mark 12:1-12/Luke 20:9-18), the Two Debtors (Luke 7:41-43), the Dishonest Steward (Matt 24:45-51; Luke 12:42-46), and the Man Going on a Journey (Mark 13:34-36)."

21 See Nick Spencer, *The Political Samaritan: How Power Hijacked a Parable* (London: Bloomsbury, 2017).

22 Some commentators believe Jesus only sought to make one point with every parable. Others fundamentally disagree and allow for a multitude of meanings. Still others argue each parable had one central point to make and may have other additional layers of meaning.

23 In Luke the servants are explicitly instructed to "do business", for profit, until the master returns.

24 Francis Wright Beare, *The Gospel According to Matthew* (Oxford: Basil Blackwell, 1981), p. 486.

25 Basil the Great, Homily on Psalm 14, 'Against usury', *www.earlychurchtexts.com/public/basil_homily_psalm_14_against_usury.htm* (Site accessed: 04/12/2018).

26 Unpublished lecture. My thanks to Bishop Graham for making this available.

27 Joan Lockwood O'Donovan, 'The Theological Economics of Medieval Usury Theory'. Studies in Christian Ethics, Vol. 14/1, 2001, p. 53.

28 *Ibid.*, p. 52.

29 Joan Lockwood O'Donovan, 'The Theological Economics of Medieval Usury Theory' in Oliver O'Donovan & Joan Lockwood O'Donovan, *Bonds of Imperfection: Christian Politics, Past and Present* (Grand Rapids, MI: Eerdmans, 2004), p. 102.

30 M. Douglas Meeks, 'The Peril of Usury in the Christian Tradition'. *Interpretation*, April 2011, pp. 131, 138.

31 The Greek word used in this Matthew passage is *teleios* and can mean perfect, but is more often used for maturity and wholeness. See Paula Gooder, 'What Does Jesus Mean when He Says "Be perfect"?', *www.biblesociety.org.uk/explore-the-bible/bible-articles/what-does-jesus-mean-when-he-says-be-perfect/* (Site accessed 28/11/2018).

32 Joan Lockwood O'Donovan, 'The Theological Economics of Medieval Usury Theory', *Studies in Christian Ethics*, Vol. 14/1, (2001), p. 61.

33 Luther as quoted by O'Donovan, ibid, p. 62.

34 John Calvin, 'Letter on Usury' (date unknown) in ed. Denis R. Janz, *A Reformation Reader: Primary Texts with Introductions*, 2nd edition (Minneapolis, MN: Fortress Press, 2008), p. 262.

35 *Ibid.*, p. 263.

36 *Ibid.*, p. 264.

37 See especially Paul Mills, 'The Ban on Interest: Dead Letter or Radical Solution?', *Cambridge Papers*, Vol. 1, No. 4 (1993); and 'The Divine Economy', *Cambridge Papers*, Vol. 9, No. 4 (2000).

38 Ben Cooper in a review of Guy Brandon, Crumbling Foundations (Cambridge, UK: Jubilee, 2016) argues that extrapolations from biblical texts "concerned with situations of borrowing as an emergency measure to survive a period of extreme poverty" to issues of debt and lending in general are unwarranted. *theceme.org/ben-cooper-crumbling-foundations-biblical-critique-modern-money-guy-brandon/* (Site accessed 28/11/2018).

39 See Guy Brandon, *Crumbling Foundations* (Cambridge, UK: Jubilee, 2016), pp. 12-21.

40 *Ibid.*, pp. 19, 41-42.

41 Paul Mills, 'The Great Financial Crisis: A biblical diagnosis', *Cambridge Papers*, Vol. 20, No. 1, 2 (2011).

42 Guy Brandon, 'Debt Slaves', *Threads* 2.1, November 2013. *www.threadsuk.com/debt-slaves* (Site accessed 28/11/2018).

43 Paul Mills, 'The Great Financial Crisis: A biblical diagnosis', *Cambridge Papers*, Vol. 20, No. 1, (2011), p. 3.

44 Paul Mills, 'The Ban on Interest: Dead Letter or Radical Solution', *www.jubilee-centre.org/the-ban-on-interest-dead-letter-or-radical-solution-by-paul-mills/* (Site accessed 28/11/2018).

45 Kathryn Tanner, *Economy of Grace* (Minneapolis: Fortress, 2005).

46 *Ibid.*, pp. 63, 72.

47 *Ibid.*, p. 75.

48 *Ibid.*, p. 31.

49 Kathryn Tanner, 'Economies of Grace', in *Having: Property and Possession in Religious and Social Life*, ed. William Schweiker and Charles Matthews (Grand Rapids, MI: Eerdmans), p. 370.

50 *Ibid.*, p. 371.

51 *Ibid.*, p. 374.

52 *Ibid.*, p. 373.

53 Luke Bretherton, *Christ and the Common Life: A Guide to Political Theology* (Grand Rapids, MI: Eerdmans, forthcoming 2019).

54 *Ibid.*

55 *Ibid.*

56 Jeremy Bentham, *Defence of Usury*, 1787 (London: Routledge, 1992 edition).

57 *Ibid.*

58 *Ibid.*

59 *Ibid.*

60 *Ibid.*

3
Debt tomorrow: lending and borrowing as if relationships matter

As Chapter 2 has demonstrated, Scripture and Christian theology have much to say about the right ordering of economic life, the moral dimensions of borrowing and lending, and the relational implications of debt. Our survey of biblical, historical and contemporary theologies has shown, however, that there is a polyphony of views on debt within the Christian tradition.

Yet if there is a polyphony, there is also – to push the metaphor further – a principal melody that can be heard within the broad Christian teaching on debt: the concern for the welfare of people, particularly the poor and marginalised; the concern to ensure all members of society are able to participate in a common life; and justice in the relations between lenders and borrowers. Starting from these principles, and drawing on the theological and moral thought surveyed in the previous chapter, we next indicate the contours of a moral framework for assessing contemporary debt in the UK.

The moral framework

Just debt

In this report we argue that debt is never merely an economic or financial issue but also a deeply moral one. It depends on judgements about what is right and fair, and who should bear the risks associated with it. These are not questions that can be answered in a neutral way or approached in a 'technocratic' fashion.

In themselves, debt and interest are neither amoral nor immoral, but morally ambivalent. Debt should be judged on the *purpose* for which it is incurred, the *terms* of the debt – whether these are clearly presented, fair and freely accepted; and the broader *consequences* for lenders and borrowers and the health of the wider society.

Christian moral teaching on debt is particularly concerned with the quality of relationships debt establishes: between lenders and borrowers primarily, but also within the wider society that is affected directly or indirectly by debt. When risk is shared by the parties involved, and when the relationship involves some measure of reciprocity, debt relations and interest are legitimate. In other words, where debt contributes, in some way, to the flourishing of both borrowers and lenders, debt is morally acceptable.

At their best, the bonds established through debt create flourishing communities and markets that can serve the common good. A position of having no debts, while eschewing promises and obligations, can be just as problematic as borrowing heavily and unsustainably.[1]

There are undeniable historic benefits of credit in the monetary economy. The history of capitalism shows that profit from interest-bearing credit and the exchanges it enables was a catalyst of wealth creation and technological development. It also continues to play a key role in enabling the provision of both state-sponsored welfare and private initiatives of welfare provision. Credit, debt and interest have also helped forge relations between strangers, even 'political enemies' who do not have a shared life.[2]

Bad debt

But there is a darker side to the story. Too often debt plays into consumerism's hollow promises[3] or is used for domination and exploitation. It is often the case that debt tends to give more power to the lender, while pushing most, if not all, costs and risks associated with the transaction onto the borrower.

The borrower is often required to provide collateral to mitigate against the risk incurred by the lender. When the borrower is unable keep up with interest payments, the collateral may be taken away.

Scripture is alert to the severity and potentially abusive nature of penalties attached to the lending/borrowing relationship. As the book of Proverbs strikingly puts it: "Do not be one of those who give pledges, who become surety for debts. If you have nothing with which to pay, why should your bed be taken from under you?" (Prov. 22:26-27). The risk, as the passage makes clear, is not only financial loss but complete disenfranchisement. But, rather than suggesting that debt is to be avoided at all times, it offers a basis for regulation. For example, today this could include interest rates capping, price capping in the rent-to-own market or extending the repayment schedule at fixed interest rates in order to make debt more sustainable,[4] to protect the parties involved – particularly the more vulnerable.

Modern debt is increasingly anonymous and impersonal. While physical distances continue to shrink through scientific and technological advancements, people are becoming increasingly alienated from each other and loneliness continues to rise.[5] While the growing anonymity of debt has the benefit of making discriminatory lending more difficult, the darker side of this is that the story of the borrower and the particular circumstances in which a loan is sought now play little part in the lender's decision to lend or not (or the terms of the loan, when this is made available). Detailed regulation that is alert to the human dimensions of lending and borrowing, and the risks and vulnerabilities therein involved, is as necessary as it is difficult to devise.

Christian teaching clearly stresses individual financial responsibility in debt and economic relations more generally. But as we have indicated in Chapter 2, it also highlights the existence of structural injustice and denounces the various forces and systems that constrict and condition individual behaviour and freedom. Saying "greed is bad" or "live within your means" and advising against certain forms of personal debt is fine moral advice, but it rings hollow if there isn't a clear recognition of the structural issues and forces at play that determine individual behaviour, constrict freedom or artificially feed human desires. These range from a government's fiscal and economic policy to pervasive and relentless marketing, not least in the area of consumer debt.

No debt?

It cannot be denied that there are countless situations in which the ability to borrow is a life and death matter. There are loans on which people's lives depend, but which borrowers are then unable to repay. Sustained and problematic debt can, and often does, lead to actual slavery. In this context it is worth remembering that, at its most basic level, the Christian faith does not teach debt repayment as its highest ethic. Rather it champions debt forgiveness. While the relationship between atonement theology and a Christian ethics of economic debt must be carefully negotiated, it is safe to say that Christianity announces liberation from the debt of sin through divine forgiveness not human repayment.

While this is undoubtedly relevant to the issue of contemporary debt – even if there is much more theological nuance that could be added – there is no shortcut to political, economic and recommendations from here. The upshot is not that all existing debts should be forgiven wholesale. Assuming this were possible in our intricate and highly interdependent modern economies, chaos would likely ensue. This is to say nothing of the resulting injustice – who should forgive and with what authority, given that, as we have seen, there are a myriad of borrower/lender relations? Attractive as it may be (to some, at least) then, the scenario of a wholesale forgiveness of debts is as impractical as it is unethical.

But not all suggestions of debt forgiveness that have been made in recent years – think of the Jubilee 2000 campaign for the cancellation of developing country debt[6] and the recent Jubilee Debt Campaign seeking a write-off of problem personal debt[7] – are comprehensive in scope. They address specific types of debt – developing world and personal problem debt, respectively – and in the former significant success has been registered. Later in this chapter we discuss further how the Christian notions of forgiveness and gift may find contemporary incarnations in the UK.

In the light of all this, and before moving on to a more focused discussion of some of the key issues and areas of concern around contemporary debt, we offer below a summary of the Christian ethics of debt put forward in this report. We suggest that debt can be just or equitable when:

- it is mutually beneficial to creditor and debtor;
- costs and risks associated with the contract are fairly distributed;
- it can be shown to foster rather than corrode relationships – among debtors, creditors and all third-parties involved;
- it enables participation in, rather than isolation from, the body politic and the common life;
- it does not overburden future generations;

— it is based on a responsible, steward-like relationship to the physical world.

Key areas of concern: from principles to practice

This next section identifies some of the key questions and areas of concern that emerged during the roundtable conversations organised as part of this research project. We have done our best to incorporate as many of the comments and suggestions from these roundtables as possible within the framework of this report, although the range of viewpoints and nature of this essay naturally preclude any comprehensiveness here. The section begins a discussion of these key questions within the moral framework provided above and seeks to apply the wisdom of the Christian tradition to our current debt predicament at the personal, business and national level.

It is difficult to do this, however, without a discussion of two subjects far larger than the topic of this essay: the kind of economic system we want, and the resultant 'shape shifting' between personal, business and national debt based upon government policy and democratic decision-making. Below is an attempt to summarise these issues briefly.

There are many possible forms of capitalism. Most recently, much of the West has experienced a neo-liberal, financialised capitalism (see text box), which makes three key presumptions:

1) Markets are the best determinant of the price of almost anything, and the value of something is determined only by the price someone will pay for it.

2) The maximisation of shareholder benefit is the purpose of business.[8]

3) Capital should be free to flow across borders in order to go wherever it can be most profitably used.

The financialisation of capitalism

Traditionally, the two key inputs in an enterprise are labour and capital, by which we mean investment in productive assets like factories, research and development and new technology. The mix of labour and capital in an enterprise will vary depending on the nature of the enterprise, how it is managed and the economic environment. In its heyday, labour had almost equivalent power to capital due to the power of the labour unions. Since the shift to a neo-liberal economy in the 1980s, power has shifted to the investor. An investor assesses a project (be it a building, a company or a government activity) not as a function of the profits of the project resulting from its capital and labour inputs, but on the total financial return of the project from both income and capital gains. With this goal in mind, it becomes important for enterprises to seek out the best sources of funding, or credit.

This change in emphasis, away from simply increasing the profit of a company towards maximising its share price, has led to a dramatic increase in companies using their profits to buy and cancel their own shares, a procedure known as "share buybacks". Environments that assist investors achieve high financial returns in this way feature low labour costs, low taxes and strong property rights, in particular intellectual property rights.

Governments compete to make their economies attractive to companies, largely by lowering taxes and reducing labour-law protections. The consequent decrease in wages and lower taxes results in lower government revenue. This in turn means that the government must borrow to replace lost tax revenues. At the extreme, governments can no longer borrow from markets because of soaring deficits and debt burdens. Reducing public debt becomes the objective, rather than maximising revenue, in order to make the economy attractive to investors who might be enticed to fund the national debt.

This, in turn, spurs the growth of personal debt.[9] If there is a decrease in real personal income, because of weaker labour bargaining power and lower government transfers to the less well off, individuals are forced to borrow to meet their needs.[10]

Neo-liberal, financialised capitalism often pays insufficient attention to several key issues:

1) Even the most conservative economists believe that regulation is needed to curb the worst of human tendencies.

2) Economic models tend to ignore externalities that result from economic activity, such as pollution and global warming.

3) While capital can flow freely, nation states have considerable concerns about letting labour (i.e. immigration) also flow freely across states. What these assumptions include and exclude have caused the capitalism of the last 50 years to veer far from core Christian principles. Our job in this chapter is to consider whether and how they might be reconciled.

As mentioned in Chapter 1, policy choices affect how debt is distributed between individuals, businesses and the government. The electorate makes choices about the basic level of service provision that should exist and the extent to which that service provision is provided directly by the private sector or by the state. This determines the total size of government in any economy. This can change at the margin as popular will and governments change. Here are just a few examples of how these changes can affect the distribution of debt within society:

— To the extent that neither wages nor social benefits are sufficient to meet basic needs of the population, the poorest members may try to borrow in order to cover daily spending.

— Decreases in tax often result in cuts in social benefits. When this happens, those earning the most tend to benefit the most. Those earning the least are doubly hit. As they pay little tax, they do not benefit from the tax cuts, yet they also suffer from the loss of social benefits.

— The shift from student grants (a form of gift) to student loans (debt) also shows how government can shift costs from themselves to the individual. This could have damaging consequences, such as directing students into subjects that promise higher earnings (finance and the technology sector), while neglecting subjects and areas that may be lower paying but are vital for a well-functioning society. It can also cause graduates to defer starting families and home ownership while they work to repay student debt, pushing back investment in time.

The following section will draw out the relationship between core theological concepts of debt and our current situation in the UK.

From 'tribe' to global community

Within the United Kingdom today, we are a multi-faith, multi-cultural group of people. Open markets and borders allow us to know what is going on around the world in real time. But these things mean we can struggle to know where to draw the lines of community. Do we draw them around our family, our village, our country, continent or the globe? The internet and economic globalisation have, in a sense, brought us closer to each other and made us more interdependent than ever before. Theologian Ilsup Ahn says: "we are now called in a different way to be keepers of near or remote strangers of this planetary community,"[11] and therefore must consider ways to apply the principles of the Jubilee provisions in ancient Israel. Specifically, Ahn argues we should treat debt as a form of gift, rather than use it to control and dominate.

Even if we acknowledge we are all made in God's image, we must recognise that we cannot know one another as those who are members of the same immediate tribe described in the Old Testament would. Nonetheless, we have noted earlier that debt is fundamentally relational, and, as such, we need to consider the relationships that networks of debt create between borrowers and lenders.

And yet, as we noted earlier, the financialisation of our economy makes those relationships increasingly distant and anonymous. The trader who buys or sells a security may go through a chain of intermediation between the ultimate owner of those funds and themselves (such chains can number anything from two to 20 people). The person whose money the trader is investing is entirely anonymous to them, yet a portion of those funds represent someone's savings for a home, or a wedding or retirement. Where once a borrower, whether an individual or a small business, went to their local bank to talk to their banker about a loan, most often now an agency provides an algorithmic credit score for that borrower, which in turn drives a credit algorithm at the bank to decide whether or not they will lend the funds. The relational aspect of debt has largely disappeared in both these examples. This is likely to worsen as Artificial Intelligence (AI) grows in usage for credit decisions by both traditional banks and new companies providing financial services through new technology, known as FinTech (see Appendix, 'FinTech: new wine in old bottles?.)

Reconciling the definition of who is within our 'known' circle, and how we treat that circle, versus the 'other' will be critical, as will re-establishing the relational nature of the borrower/lender arrangement.

Avoiding abuse

While it may be tempting to yearn for a past of local banks and local bankers, it is important to remember that in those halcyon days, credit was strictly rationed and hard to come by for most people. We must be mindful that more widespread access to credit has benefits as well as detriments, all the while ensuring that we maintain fairness in the allocation of credit and do not permit either discrimination or differentiated treatment that penalises the poor. This means ensuring access to borrowing where that access is warranted, such that those most able to pay, pay most. It is critical that banks be held accountable for those to whom they lend. Resolution depends on issues of 'fairness,' not a term traditionally associated with pure market finance, but one that does need to be restored to the vocabulary of financial markets.[12]

This means that we need to re-establish reciprocal relations between borrower and lender in order to ensure the lender understands the borrower's circumstances and the borrower understands the terms on which he or she is receiving the money. Already in the United Kingdom, the Financial Conduct Authority works to prevent customer abuse and a chain of agencies, including the Financial Ombudsman Service,[13] provide recourse for those who feel they have been mistreated. In an ideal world, financial institutions would understand and integrate these responsibilities into their operations. Where they do not, the regulator exists to enforce these behaviours.[14]

Balance of power

Debt contracts need to be both mutually beneficial and protective so that the privileged positions of lenders, with more information, does not allow them to take advantage of those with less (this is known as information asymmetry). In addition, new ways of ensuring risk is equitably shared must be found. In all this, the disproportionate power institutional lenders have over individual borrowers must be counterbalanced.

Regulations and regulators exist as a counterbalance to the asymmetry of information and power. Together with the courts they have required banks to pay out over £25 billion to over 12 million customers who held payment protection insurance (PPI) in one of the biggest mis-selling scandals in British banking history.[15] Of course, this asymmetry can also be reversed by the amount borrowed. There is a joke that goes: "if I owe the bank £1,000, I have a problem. However, if I owe the bank £10 million, the bank has a problem."

Stewardship

We all bear the responsibility of caring for God's creation. However, as we have seen above, the economic model we live with does not have a straightforward means of pricing the harm we do to creation, and, as such, this is often ignored (this is known as integrating 'externalities'). We need a new model that incorporates these costs within our financial transactions. Investor activism is making some inroads here. In particular, the Ethical Investment Advisory Group (EIAG) of the Church of England, among others, works to apply its theologically based views to the investments it makes with the Church's money. This model must include provision for those who cannot provide for themselves: the poor, the aged and the infirm. It must actively encourage investment in things that support and nurture the common good, such as education and infrastructure.

Intergenerational equity

Intergenerational equity is closely related to stewardship insofar as those currently alive have an obligation to leave a world for the next generation where they can thrive. The principle of intergenerational justice demands that one generation must not benefit or suffer unfairly at the cost of another. By definition, future generations cannot participate in the contemporary democratic process to deliberate on tax levels, yet through excessive debt financing of public spending they have to shoulder the burden.

The challenge for this level of the discussion of debt is to go beyond the moralistic handwringing around intergenerational fairness to consider how we devise policies, fiscal and otherwise, that are fair towards both older and future generations. Were we only to look at the debt burden passed on, we would neglect technological advances, changes in longevity and other benefits the current population is bequeathing to future generations.

From a debt perspective, a position of intergenerational equity may be achieved when debt is taken on to help protect creation, create systems that reduce existential threats,[16] or establish systems that enhance the conditions for thriving of future generations: health, education, disease-control and others. This, however, requires the recovery of a sense of solidarity with, and responsibility towards, future generations.

There is wide agreement that too much government debt is economically and ethically problematic. Disagreements appear, however, around the means for reducing it and for dealing, more broadly, with the long-term sustainability of a country's tax and spending policy. The crux of the issue is the proper balancing of increased taxes and reduced government spending. The tendency to live with what Nobel Prize laureate James Buchanan called "fiscal illusion" may explain why debt has generally been preferred over taxation.[17]

Forgiveness

Debt forgiveness is an integral part of a theology of debt. Indeed, the very concept of bankruptcy, where debts are forgiven or written off, can be seen as an outworking of this Christian principle. More recently, at the personal level, the use of Individual Voluntary Agreements (IVAs) permits the reduction, if not entire forgiveness, of debt for individuals who find themselves in situations where they cannot meet their debt burdens.

It behoves us to remember the origins of these systems in our culture, and take away some of the stigma that still adheres to having to declare bankruptcy or apply for an IVA. We would be well served to embrace such systems as means of resetting, embracing and enabling a fresh start for borrowers, even if this results in the well-off bearing a slightly higher cost of credit,

Moreover, lenders should regularly consider the advantages of forbearance – helping a borrower work through a difficult period – as a better means of recovery than foreclosure.

Gift

Related to forgiveness is the concept of gift. Luke Bretherton reminds us we should not imagine a strict dichotomy between gift and debt, 'giftfulness' and lending. As anthropologists David Graeber and Marcel Mauss show,[18] gift and debt are much closer together in archaic societies and are part of a moral economy which "engenders social and symbolic capital that [makes] possible social cohesion and solidarity."[19] The contemporary context, however, where debt continues to proliferate, stands in stark contrast to this. While not drawing a clear separation between gift and debt, it is worth remembering Christian thought gives pride of place to gifting over lending. 'Giftfulness' gives rise to reciprocity in a way that debt does not. It is also without the risk of domination, which is largely absent in gifting.

If our intention is to foster community and the common good, then it is important to remember that we each have an obligation to help the less fortunate. Regardless of the breadth of access to debt for the poor, this in no way replaces the need for charity, whether this is in the form charitable debt forgiveness, or in grants that permit those less able to repay their debts or to avoid having to borrow at all.

Recommendations

In this final section we offer a series of recommendations and steps to be taken by individuals, churches, public and private bodies, regulators and policy makers to address some of the ethically problematic features of modern debt at the personal, corporate and public levels. These range from

Debt tomorrow: lending and borrowing as if relationships matter

personal actions to nationwide changes and are organised by their focus area and the level of change they seek to effect: *formation* of lenders and borrowers; better *communication* between borrowers, lenders, third parties and the wider society on debt issues; *mitigation* against harmful and problematic debt relations; and *reformation* – initiatives that seek a more radical change of the existing system and offer alternative ways of organising our economic life and debt relations.

Formation

Formation includes, but is greater than, education. It is certainly greater than merely inculcating the right ideas. It has to do with practices that, when repeated, shape us into people for whom 'doing what is right' comes naturally. Debt problems can and should be tackled with the right economic and fiscal measures. But without virtues such as honesty, prudence, patience, concern for the other, embodied by borrowers and lenders alike at all levels, positive change achieved through technocratic and political means is at best temporary. Just as it is sometimes said that 'culture eats strategy for breakfast', character, or its lack thereof, beats regulation every time. As Ilsup Ahn puts it: "Without the proper formation of virtues among financial leaders, agents, and regulators as well as among ordinary citizens and residents, with only systemic and regulatory changes, we cannot fully realise the moral economy of debt."[20] In other words, it is only by cultivating virtue, or habits of doing the good in all situations, that we can move towards debt relations oriented towards the common good, where borrowing and lending are practices embedded within social relations and shaped by moral considerations.

1. Practically, we must improve the financial education of borrowers, both individuals and small business owners. Putting basic budgeting and interest rate calculation

in the national curriculum would be a first step. This could be done with the help of many of the debt advisory charities, such as Christians Against Poverty (CAP) and StepChange, which already do such work with individuals.

2. In addition, those who act in the market as traders need to be trained to understand that they are working on behalf of their clients, not themselves. They need to be able to see through the chain of intermediation to the ultimate beneficiary. They need always to consider transaction for both mutual benefit and whether they would be willing to sell a product to a family member (the 'Granny test'). However attractive it might be to try and break the chain of intermediation, let us as a first step ensure that all those who work in financial services are aware of their fiduciary responsibilities to those whose money they are using.

3. Churches should consider developing and running courses on the formation of desire and character to counter what Kathryn Tanner calls the 'disciplining' effects of capitalism and consumerism. These would aim at instilling the virtues of simplicity, frugality and generosity to counter the insatiable wants and desires for things and profit that run through our culture. Drawing on existing resources or developing new ones, churches should run theologically informed courses on financial stewardship. Opportunities for partnerships with organisations such as CAP should be explored.

Communication

If we are to see a return to relational lending and borrowing, an important step in that direction is to ensure greater availability, accessibility and clarity of financial information about lenders, borrowers and the debt contracts established between them. Below are a series of recommendations relevant to this point:

1. The government or the Office of Budget Responsibility (OBR) needs to make information available for every measure taken on tax and benefits, about how these measures affect directly and indirectly:

    — the poorest in the country and income distribution more generally;
    — externalities such as climate change and pollution;
    — intergenerational fairness.

    While the Office for Budget Responsibility publishes forecasts and independent analyses of public finances, the government should do more to stimulate public conversation and facilitate democratic involvement in decisions around public debt. The public needs not only to be properly informed, but also encouraged to participate in public consultation around questions such as: what do they see as responsibilities the government should undertake and what kind of tax burden are they willing to bear for them? What is the debt being used for? Almost all this information is already publicly available but needs to be presented in a form that is understandable to the general public.

2. A regular reporting that looks at, on the one hand, the debt burden for future generations, and on the other, what this might mean in terms of tax load for those who will be paying the taxes should be made public. This should then be measured against the stock of public assets from which the future generation will benefit. Ideally, both positive and negative changes passed on to

future generations would also be incorporated. On the positive side, these would include innovations and life extending and enhancing technologies. On the negative side, these would include detrimental changes to the physical environment, such as global warming, pollution and loss of species diversity. Given the enormity of this responsibility, and the number of organisations working on various angles to these subjects already, the key task will be coordination and dissemination of the data.

3   Society must be able to hold lending institutions to account; the operations of these institutions must be transparent and described in language that is accessible for the non-specialist. This will probably mean institutions need to create two different reports – one for the sophisticated investor and investor analyst, and another for the individual saver or policyholder.

4   Appropriate public consultation forums should be organised regularly, in order to discuss whether what the government commits in terms of debt is at sustainable levels and accomplishing what it was intended to do. Steps should be taken to encourage greater democratic participation in deliberations on the purpose, scope and terms of the debt taken on by the government. At the same time, where moves by government push borrowing out to the corporate or personal level, the extent and efficiency of this should also be open to public discussion.

5   Regulation should begin from the recognition that markets ought to serve social relations and society not vice versa. The market exists as a social construct for offering mutual care and assistance.[21] Regulators' aims to this end should be clearly stated. Regulations and

regulatory proposals should begin by explaining how they support society, and be regularly tested against this once enacted. Policy and regulation should reflect an ethic geared towards fairness, equity and with a particular concern for the poor and vulnerable.

6   Transactions with individuals and small business must be communicated and documented in language entirely understandable to the person undertaking the loan. Moreover, there should be a clear demonstration of the benefit to each party in the contract and the protections offered to the individual. It is worth considering whether the United Kingdom's financial regulators should adopt something for borrowers that is akin to the sophisticated and unsophisticated investor distinction drawn by the US Securities Exchange Commission (SEC)[22] for defining what information needs and what products can be sold to different types of investors.

Mitigation

Mitigation refers to actions that could be taken to relieve the burdens of the existing system, and reshape it, without wholesale upheaval and disruption. Many of these recommendations try to apply Christian principles on debt and forgiveness to existing situations.

1   Debt forgiveness should be used wherever appropriate. At the personal level this includes Individual Voluntary Arrangements (IVAs). At the small business level, bankruptcy should be a less stigmatised and more viable option. At national level debt, both debt forgiveness for the poorest countries and a bankruptcy system that works for nation states should be in place – the latter is something long discussed but not yet enacted by the

International Monetary Fund.[23] We need to embrace the principle and the spirit of Jubilee, if not the letter. The intention is to reset the counter, embrace and enable a fresh start that helps to recognise that we have a responsibility to one another and that we are all in this together. Where complete forgiveness is difficult to implement, the burden sharing evidenced by IVAs works as a good starting point.

2. Lending within or among a community at low/no interest should be encouraged. Interest may be morally legitimate for those who are unknown to us, but usurious rates of interest are never legitimate when we live in community with others. Consideration might be given to re-establishing a usury rate, or upper limit, to interest rates that may be charged by regulated institutions.

3. Stakeholder consciousness needs to increase. Managers need to think about social responsibility, as it is a key portion of a company's reputational capital. At the same time, investors who supply the money lent need to hold companies to account – as well as be held to account themselves. While some lenders and investors have clear policies on socially responsible behaviour, this is much more common for those who own equity stakes than for lenders. The same environmental, social and governance considerations should be extended to debt investors, who, in turn, need to hold companies to account. It would be similarly desirable to find a way for individuals who lend (via personal savings and pensions) to voice their view on how these funds can and should be used in pursuit of the common good. Socially responsible investment funds go some way toward this, but fund managers need to find

ways that small savers can have more of a voice in how their money is used.

4. In the same way, investors in government debt need to use their power to change government policy, as must taxpayers. At the extreme end, debtors could unite, such as those who owe student debt, to threaten wholesale default, in order to force a reconsideration of student debt terms.

5. It would be beneficial to re-establish the cooperative model at all levels of society.[24] This movement would permit workers to have an interest in the profits of the place they work at as co-owners. It would give them more power over the rates they are paid for their work as well as their benefits. This would hopefully limit the need for month-end borrowings in order to make ends meet. Interestingly, there is already a movement afoot among workers in the gig economy to this end.[25]

6. In the 2018 Autumn Budget statement, the Chancellor of the Exchequer, Phillip Hammond, announced that government would partner with debt charities and the banking industry to launch a feasibility study to help those on lower salaries pay for life's unexpected costs.[26] The Budget states that:

> *A strong and vibrant social lending sector is crucial so that everyone has access to valuable financial services, regardless of their circumstances. Following the work of the Financial Inclusion Policy Forum, the Budget announces new policies to help households manage unexpected costs by increasing access to fair and affordable credit, as well as a consultation on a breathing space scheme for people who fall into problem debt.*[27]

"Forgive Us Our Debts"

>These measures should be strongly supported by all who care about just finance.
>
>7   The embedding of credit unions within church communities presents important advantages. Relations are more personal – people generally know each other by name – and power-imbalances between lenders and borrowers are corrected "as members who are net borrowers serve savers in other ways, such as giving their time to a Sunday school or sports club".[28]
>
>8   In order to help bring about a return to relational borrowing and lending, where borrowers have established relationships with lenders, consideration should be given to preferential loan pricing.
>
>9   Without restricting the ability of individuals to access credit, restricting consumer credit advertising (particularly credit card and payday loans) may be beneficial in the same way that restrictions exist on advertising other products considered harmful, such as tobacco, sports gambling and even sweets for children.
>
>10 In a clear example of debt shifting, austerity policies have limited central government transfers to local authorities, causing them in turn to tighten collections policies.[29] We strongly support current efforts to stop local authorities sending in bailiffs to individuals for non-payment of local rates.

Reformation

If mitigation softens the burden of the current system, this section on reformation calls for more radical change, though the recommendations fall well short of calling for either the forgiveness of all debt, or the overthrow of the current economic system.

1. Corporate debt should be put on an equal tax footing with equity. This means eliminating the tax deductibility of debt as well as considering the elimination of the tax on corporate dividends. Removing debt interest tax deductibility without doing something on the taxation of dividends would be difficult given the considerable opposition to such a change by shareholders. There has been little or no new equity raised on public markets in recent years and the number of publicly quoted companies[30] is dropping fast. Work needs to be done on the extent to which this is a result of tax treatment versus a conscious choice to use the private equity route. Private equity limits public disclosure and the resultant public and regulatory scrutiny.[31]

2. Consideration should be given to rethinking UK university tuition loans. Introduction of needs-based financing needs to be explored. There are several ways to do this: scalar interest rates based on financial need, interest free loans or free tuition to the least able to pay are all possibilities

3. We should consider moving towards a situation where those most able to pay the most interest do so, while those least able to pay, pay the least (this is, in fact, the opposite of the current situation). The excess interest paid by those most able to afford it would then subsidise those who could not.

Fundamental to all this is for all of us to raise the beginner questions of 'for whom' and 'for what purpose' should our economic lives be organised. These are the major questions our society needs to ask as the starting points for fundamental structural change in both issues of debt, and the economy more generally.[32]

4   We should encourage greater involvement in democratic, grassroots, cooperative economic arrangements and initiatives. These include: town hall economic consultations, credit unions (church-led/based), community banking, regional banks, Local Exchange Trading Schemes (LETS) and consumer associations, as well as, more generally, community land trusts, social enterprises and other initiatives springing from community organising. Associational practices of 'democratic citizenship' at the level of production, distribution and exchange can effectively mitigate against the "toxic effects of debt and its use to control and manage the indebted".[33] These efforts disperse and share power, and help foster community and relation building, as well as acting as an alternative and counterbalance to corporate power. The Church has been making laudable efforts on this front through initiatives such as church-based credit unions and social lending, but there is ample room for growth and innovation.

As we have shown in this report, Christianity has much to say about making debt relations fairer and more aligned with the common good. Indeed, the Christian ideal is not necessarily a completely debt-free society, but one in which lending occurs in relationships of mutuality and gift exchange. The Church, in all of its denominational variety, has a unique responsibility and opportunity around debt problems today to model an alternative economic life based on generosity rather than scarcity, on trust rather than credit score, on relationships of reciprocity rather than domination and exploitation. As

M. Douglas Meeks puts it, "in the question of usury, the most important contribution the church can make is to witness to God's transforming economy of grace."[34] Or as Bishop Graham Tomlin says, the Church has a unique opportunity to signpost an alternative, better way of relating in society, and model "an economy based on the needs of others, and on a basic ethic of generosity and trust".[35]

1 Germany's net creditor position can be considered as an example of this.

2 Luke Bretherton, "'Love Your Enemies': Usury, Citizenship and the Friend-Enemy Distinction", *Modern Theology* Vol. 27/3, 2011, p. 381.

3 Eve Poole, 'Death-defying handbags'. www.theosthinktank.co.uk/comment/2018/11/20/deathdefying-handbags (Site accessed 29/11/2018).

4 For more information on price capping see: www.fca.org.uk/publications/consultation-papers/cp18-35-rent-own-alternatives-high-cost-credit-feedback-cp18-12-consultation-price-cap (Site accessed 29/11/2018).

5 "Loneliness is pervasive and rising, particularly among the young", *The Economist*, 31 August 2018. www.economist.com/graphic-detail/2018/08/31/loneliness-is-pervasive-and-rising-particularly-among-the-young (Site accessed 29/11/2018).

6 See Ann Pettifor, 'The Jubilee 2000 Campaign: A Brief Overview' in eds. Chris Jochnick and Fraser A. Preston. *Sovereign Debt at the Crossroads: Challenges and Proposals for Resolving the Third World Debt Crisis* (Oxford, UK: Oxford University Press, 2006).

7 https://www.theguardian.com/money/2018/mar/05/jubilee-debt-campaign-seeks-40bn-write-off-britain-consumer-borrowing (Site accessed 29/11/2018).

8 Milton Friedman, 'The Social Responsibility of Business is to Increase its Profits', *The New York Times Magazine*, 13 September 1970.

9 On shifting the debt burden from the public sector to individuals and households, see Colin Crouch, 'Privatised Keynesianism: An Unacknowledged Policy Regime', *The British Journal of Politics & International Relations*, Vol. 11.3 (2009), pp. 382–99.

10 This text box depends largely on Michel Feher's *Rated Agency: Investee Politics in a Speculative Age*, (Brooklyn, NY: Zone Books, 2018), and Kathryn Tanner's 'Inequality and Finance-Dominated Capitalism: Recommendations for Further Reading,' *Anglican Theological Review*, Vol. 98.1, (2016), pp. 157-173.

11 Ilsup Ahn, *Just Debt: Theology, Ethics, and Neoliberalism* (Waco, TX: Baylor University Press, 2017), p. 125.

12 See Bank of England (BOE), Her Majesty's Treasury (HMT) and the Financial Conduct Authority (FCA)'s joint work on *Fair and Effective Markets*, 10 June 2015, www.bankofengland.co.uk/report/2015/fair-and-effective-markets-review---final-report (Site accessed 30/11/2018).

13 https://financial-ombudsman.org.uk/

14 See the role of the FCA and the Banking Standards Board (BSB) on this subject.

15 www.thisismoney.co.uk/money/news/article-3833245/Banks-snatching-PPI-payouts-ve-paid-25bn-years-mis-selling-say-mistakes.html (Site accessed 29/11/2018).

16 Note that this can be not only climate change issues, but also defense and peace-keeping investments.

17 James M. Buchanan, 'Public Debt, Cost Theory, and the Fiscal Illusion' in *Public Debt and Future Generations*. Ed. James M. Ferguson. (Chapel Hill, NC: University of North Carolina Press, 1964), pp. 150-63.

18 David Graeber, *Debt: The First 5000 Years* (London: Melville House, 2014 edition); Marcel Mauss, *The Gift: Forms and Functions of Exchange and Archaic Societies* trans. Ian Cunnison (Glencoe, Ill.: Free Press, 1954).

19 Ilsup Ahn, *Just Debt: Theology, Ethics, and Neoliberalism* (Waco, TX: Baylor University Press, 2017).

20 Ilsup Ahn, Just Debt: *Theology, Ethics, and Neoliberalism* (Waco, TX: Baylor University Press, 2017), p. 149.

21 Luke Bretherton, *Christ and the Common Life: Political Theology and the Case for Democracy* (Grand Rapids, MI: Eerdmans, forthcoming 2019).

22 *www.investopedia.com/terms/s/sophisticatedinvestor.asp* (Site accessed 3/12/2018).

23 *www.questia.com/library/journal/1G1-98078701/a-critique-of-sovereign-bankruptcy-initiatives-the* (Site accessed 29/11/2018).

24 'Co-operatives get new lease of life as contract workers join up.' *Financial Times*, 2 November 2018 *www.ft.com/content/9786108a-9cb6-11e8-88de-49c908b1f264* (Site checked 2/11/2018).

25 The 'gig' or 'precarious' economy is used to refer to those working without fixed term contracts, often at multiple jobs without any benefits such as paid holiday, pensions etc.

26 See Budget Red Book and the Chancellor's Budget speech from 29 October 2018 at *www.gov.uk/government/topical-events/budget-2018* (Site accessed 29/11/2018). See also the experience in Australia of Good Shepherd Microfinance on which this concept is based, *www.goodshepherdmicrofinance.org.au* (site accessed 3/12/2018)

27 *Ibid*.

28 *Ibid*.

29 Miles Brignall, 'MPs rebuke councillors for "overzealous" use of bailiffs', The Guardian, 26 July 2018, *https://www.theguardian.com/money/2018/jul/26/mps-rebuke-councils-for-overzealous-use-of-bailiffs* (Site accessed 29/11/2018).

30 Companies whose shares can be freely bought and sold on the open market.

31 Simon Johnson, 'Tax Reform and the Tax Treatment of Debt and Equity', *Peterson Institute for International Economics*, 13 July 2011, *piie.com/commentary/*

testimonies/tax-reform-and-tax-treatment-debt-and-equity (Site accessed 29/11/2018).

32 Kathryn Tanner, *Economy of Grace* (Minneapolis: Fortress, 2005), p. 173.

33 Luke Bretherton, *Resurrecting Democracy: Faith, Citizenship, and the Politics of a Common Life* (Cambridge: Cambridge University Press, 2015), p. 251.

34 M. Douglas Meeks, 'The Peril of Usury in the Christian Tradition'. *Interpretation*, April 2011, p. 140.

35 Unpublished lecture.

Appendix

Did the Jubilee ever happen?
According to Leviticus 25, Israel was to celebrate the year of the Jubilee after 49 Sabbath years (7 x 7 – Ex. 21:2). The Jubilee legislation demanded three things: the cancellation of all debts, the release of debt slaves and the return of the land to its original owners. Until recently, there was some uncertainty, in academia and beyond, whether the Jubilee was more than an ideal and therefore if it was ever practiced.[1]

More recent scholarship, however, decisively shows that cancellation of personal debts (agrarian debts and arrears),[2] liberation of bondservants, and the return of the land to its original owners occurred regularly in the ancient Near East from 2500 BC, in Sumer, to 1600 BC, in Babylonia and its neighbours, then in Assyria in the first millennium BC.[3] New rulers taking to the throne would engage in these practices to restore social, economic and military stability in their lands.

Drawing on extensive historical research and archaeological evidence, economic historian Michael Hudson argues that Judaism formalised the practices now associated with the Jubilee Year. It took them out of the hands of fickly worldly rulers and placed them within a strong ethical basis and at the heart of its formal teaching.[4] The Jubilee, Hudson argues, became "the defining act of Jewish post-exilic identity".[5]

Debt and sin
The relationship of debt to sin in the Bible is subtle. According to the Lord's prayer in Matthew 6, sin is described as a debt. One extreme to be avoided is to think the juxtaposition of sin and debt is arbitrary. The other is to see an equivalence between the two.

To make debt and sin equivalent and conclude all debt is sin is to fail to appreciate the way biblical language operates and the particular economic context for this biblical language. In mentioning the economic context of the Old Testament and New Testament we are not denying that there are important continuities between the economic system in biblical times and our modern economic system. The powerful continue to oppress the weak, often through the mechanism of debt. But just as there are elements of continuity, there are also differences. We must stay alert to these.

Rather than reading equivalence between debt and sin, seeing debt as an analogy for sin is more promising. Sin acts like a bad debt which promises much more than it delivers. It comes with unfair, often hidden, terms, and with levels of interest and fees that make repayment virtually impossible. It ends up keeping the borrower in a perpetual state of indebtedness or debt bondage. At first attractive, both sin and unfair debt end up enslaving and crushing the borrower.

Another analogy that can be drawn is between ruthless lenders and the human captivity to sin. As an enslaving force commandeered by quasi-personal powers and principalities (Eph. 6:12), sin behaves like a ruthless lender who makes it impossible for the borrower to free herself or himself (Rom. 5:12-13; 8:2,4).

Free to borrow?

At one level the person going into debt does so voluntarily by getting a credit card, a loan, mortgage etc. He or she freely enters into a contractual relationship that specifies rights and obligations. There is no physical coercion therefore the person is free. There are problems with this view, as the below illustration reveals.

Is a single mother on a zero-hours contract, who can't make ends meet, truly free when she clicks through to the online payday lender's website? There is no physical coercion but it is clear that this is not a contract she enters into freely, in any meaningful sense of the word, but rather she does so under duress. If she takes on the payday loan with an extortionate level of interest, which she can probably never pay off, she is in effect in debt bondage.

Such instances as the illustration above show the troubling features of a contractual view of citizenship. In this view people are assumed to be autonomous, fully rational, utility-maximising individuals who enter into such commercial contracts with full knowledge of the terms and conditions, down to the small print, and their personal motivations and possibilities for paying it off. Contracts assume by default equality between borrower and lender. This is patently not (always) the case. It is generally the case that lenders have greater power, not just monetary (by definition) but also cultural and legal power. These instances show how power can be exercised "in a wholly accountable, nonarbitrary manner without physical coercion and on the basis of a presumed equality, yet it can entirely strip one of dignity and recognition as a fellow human."[6]

Payday lenders know what the effects of their terms will have on the borrower, but keep silent because a borrower unable to pay interest, let alone pay off the principal, is 'good for business', as the interest and fees compound. The borrower is literally enslaved. In such cases we instinctively know we are faced with an injustice even if the loan has been taken legally and (supposedly) voluntarily.

Added to this is the problem of marketing and advertising. Put simply, intense and pervasive advertising in all corners of the public space feeds and determines human desires and wants, driving excessive consumption or making what turns out be a vicious predatory loan attractive and easy to secure.

With GDP tethered to consumption, and still reigning supreme as the preferred metric for the health of an economy, the high levels of consumer debt come as no surprise.

FinTech: new wine in old bottles?

New developments in financial technology (FinTech) have both attractive and potentially damaging possibilities for the indebted consumer or household. FinTech has been praised in some quarters for drawing attention to the link between mental health issues and the challenge of keeping on top of personal finances, with developments such as the creation of tools designed to help people self-diagnose mental health problems while exercising better control over their finances during tough times.[7] At the low technology end, pre-loaded credit cards permit users to spend up to the amount on the card, without increasing their debt load. This can permit those without access to credit to buy goods where card payment is required, enabling them to access lower cost products. New developments also permit the use of budgeting tools, which may help people better keep track of what they can afford. These tools can also be used to load debit cards with the amount the consumer can afford to spend.

Apps such as Mint and Goodbudget are designed to help keep track of personal debts and budgets by showing monthly spending alongside the status of debts in real time, whether via credit cards or student loans. They can also help to compartmentalise money by doing the electronic equivalent of keeping some money in jars or envelopes, encouraging the setting aside of funds for certain purposes. Other apps, such as Level Money, show how much a user can spend if they wish to be able to save. In short, apps can give individuals a sense of how much money they actually possess.[8]

However the marriage between FinTech and personal finance doesn't always produce positive outcomes. The greatest fear is that the collection of personal data may permit lenders to personalise interest rates to the detriment of the borrower, much in the manner that some websites raise travel rates on flights or hotels that a computer is accessing regularly. Access to such data may also make lenders aware of personal spending habits or histories, resulting in lenders effectively blackballing such customers. It is too early to tell whether these products are simply 'old wine in new bottles' because, as these firms grow in size and importance they will have many of the same vulnerabilities as traditional lenders in terms of credit risk, managing their assets and liabilities, and risks of interest rate and credit demand cycles despite being posited as a more efficient alternative to banks.[9]

Other innovations in this century have included peer-to-peer lending and crowd funding. At the household level, peer-to-peer lending and micro-credit are largely interchangeable terms suggesting a system, localised or web-based, where groups of individuals use their small amounts of savings to lend to each other in turn. In many ways this is a return to the old friendly society or building society system of community lending. It is most common among those without access to bank credit; at the localised level this concept works on relational principles so that savers are supporting their friendship group, family group or a particular community or social grouping.

Crowd funding is often used for small business start-ups that would not be considered by traditional banks. In such cases an entrepreneur 'sells' his or her idea on a social media platform and people contribute funds in exchange for products, services, an ownership interest or, occasionally, purely to support the new venture. It can also be used to publicise specific needs, such as funding acute medical care, but is not generally a personal finance tool.

While workplace-based or salary-based lending has long been used in limited circumstances in the UK, such as for travel cards or further education, it has not been as widely used as in other countries, notably the United States where employee credit unions are widespread.[10]

1 See, for example, Gordon J. Wenham, *The Book of Leviticus*. The New International Commentary on the Old Testament, eds. R. K. Harrison and Robert L. Hubbard, Jr. (Grand Rapids, MI: Eerdmans, 1979). Kindle location: 651.3/759.

2 Commercial debt was not cancelled as part of the 'clean slate' policy.

3 Michael Hudson, *...and forgive them their debts: lending, foreclosure and redemption from Bronze Age Finance to the Jubilee Year* (Dresden: ISLET-Verlag, 2018), p. ix.

4 Ibid., p. 7.

5 Ibid., p. 208.

6 Bretherton, *Resurrecting Democracy: Faith, Citizenship, and the Politics of a Common Life* (Cambridge: Cambridge University Press, 2015), p. 255.

7 Nick Cherry, 'How fintech can support people with mental health problems – and what the collections sector needs to do', CSA, 2 August 2017, *www.csa-uk.com/news/news.asp?id=381195&hh* (Site accessed 30/11/2018).

8 Nikolai Kuznetsov, 'Fintech Gets Serious About Personal Finance', *Forbes*, 21 April 2017, *www.forbes.com/sites/nikolaikuznetsov/2017/04/21/fintech-gets-serious-about-personal-finance/* (Site accessed 30/1//2018).

9 John Gapper, 'Financial Times Cracks are appearing in fintech lenders', *Financial Times*, 11 May 2016, *www.ft.com/content/028be304-1759-11e6-b197-a4af20d5575e* (Site accessed 30/11/2018).

10 For more on this see Mark Morrin, 'Credit Emancipation: How salary-linked lending can help turn around disadvantaged places', ResPublica, 12 September 2018, *www.respublica.org.uk/our-work/publications/credit-emancipation-making-communities-more-prosperous-and-productive/* (Site accessed 30/11/2018).

6

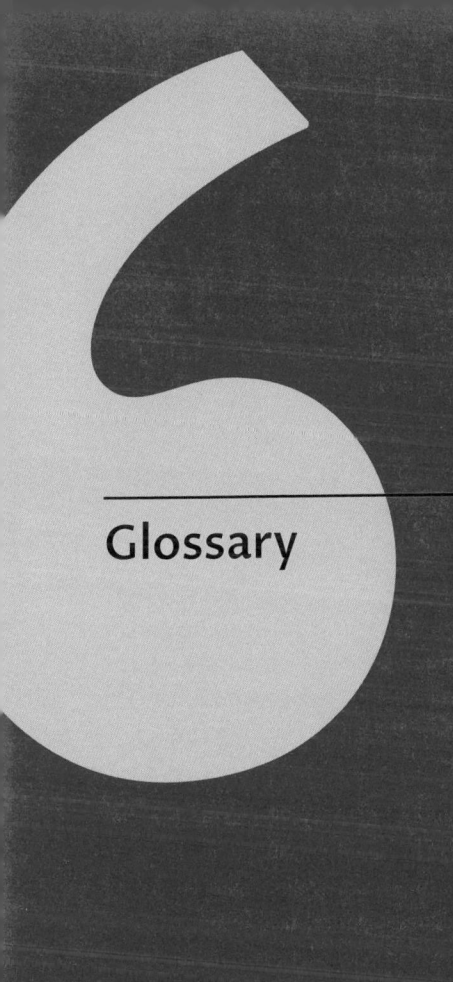

Glossary

Austerity: A political-economic term referring to policies that aim to reduce government budget deficits through spending cuts, tax increases, or a combination of both.

Bond: A bond is an interest paying instrument that represents a loan made by an investor to a borrower. It can be thought of as an I.O.U. between the lender and borrower that includes the details of the loan and its payments.

Corporate finance: Corporate finance concerns a company's financial and investment decisions. It is primarily concerned with maximising value to shareholders through long-term and short-term financial planning and the implementation of various strategies.

Factoring: This describes funding source that agrees to pay a company the value of an invoice less a discount for commission and fees. The factor advances most of the invoiced amount to the company immediately, and the balance upon receipt of funds from the invoiced party.

Financial Ombudsman Service: This is a public advocate body that was established in 2000 to help settle disputes between consumers and UK-based businesses providing financial services, such as banks, building societies, insurance companies, investment firms, financial advisers and finance companies.

Fiscal policy: This is the use of government revenue collection (mainly taxes) and expenditure (spending) to influence the economy.

Gross Domestic Product (GDP): GDP is a monetary measure of the market value of all the final goods and services produced in a period of time, often annually or quarterly in a country or region.

Hire-purchase and installment sales: Hire purchase is an arrangement for buying consumer goods on credit, where the buyer makes an initial down payment, with the balance being paid in installments plus interest. It is similar to an installment plan, except, unlike installment plans, where the buyer gets the ownership rights as soon as the contract is signed with the seller, the ownership of the merchandise is not officially transferred to the buyer until all of the payments have been made.

Individual Voluntary Arrangement (IVA): This is a formal alternative for individuals wishing to avoid bankruptcy. The IVA was established by and is also governed by the Insolvency Act 1986 and constitutes a formal repayment proposal presented to a debtor's creditors via an insolvency practitioner.

Inflation: This is the rate at which the general level of prices for goods and services is rising and, consequently, the purchasing power of currency is falling.

Information asymmetry: Information asymmetry involves transactions where one party has more or better information than the other. This asymmetry creates an imbalance of power in transactions.

International Monetary Fund (IMF): The IMF, founded at the Bretton Woods Conference in 1944, is the official organisation for securing international monetary cooperation.

Investor: An investor is any person who commits funds with the expectation of financial returns. Investors use investments to grow their money and/or provide an income for future use. They can be individuals, institutions, charities or funds.

Keynesian economic policy: This term refers to when the government changes the levels of taxation and government spending in order to influence the level of economic activity.

Nominal versus real interest rates: The nominal interest rate (also known as an Annualised Percentage Rate or APR) is the periodic interest rate multiplied by the number of periods per year. The real interest rate is the nominal interest rate adjusted for the change in prices, or inflation. Any monetary price or rate, adjusted for inflation, is called the real rate. Any price or rate expressed in current terms is called the nominal price or rate.

Office of Budgetary Responsibility (OBR): The OBR is an advisory non-departmental public body that the UK government established officially in 2010 to provide independent economic forecasts and independent analysis of the public finances as background to the preparation of the UK budget.

Opportunity cost: This term describes the value of a choice, relative to an alternative. In finance it is the value that can be gained by placing money without risk.

Publicly quoted company: This is an organisation formed to carry on business that can issue shares of stock to raise funds with which to start a business or increase its capital. These shares can be bought and sold by the public at a price that changes with the value of the company and is published regularly on a public exchange.

Shares: These are units of account for various investments. The term often means the stock of a corporation, but is also used for interests in other collective investments.

Socially Responsible Investment (SRI): SRI, also known as social investment, sustainable, socially conscious, "green" or ethical investing, is any investment strategy that seeks to consider both financial return and social/environmental good to bring about a positive change.

Value-added tax (VAT): This is a consumption tax placed on a product whenever value is added at each stage of the supply chain, from production to the point of sale.

Variable or floating interest rates versus fixed: A variable, or floating interest rate loan is a loan in which the interest rate charged on the outstanding balance varies as market interest rates change. As a result, payments can go up or down over time. Fixed interest rate loans are loans in which the interest rate charged on the loan will remain fixed for all or a part of that loan's entire term, no matter what market interest rates do. This will result in your payments being the same over the term of the fixed rate.

Theos – enriching conversations

Theos exists to enrich the conversation about the role of faith in society.

Religion and faith have become key public issues in this century, nationally and globally. As our society grows more religiously diverse, we must grapple with religion as a significant force in public life. All too often, though, opinions in this area are reactionary or ill informed.

We exist to change this

We want to help people move beyond common misconceptions about faith and religion, behind the headlines and beneath the surface. Our rigorous approach gives us the ability to express informed views with confidence and clarity.

As the UK's leading religion and society think tank, we reach millions of people with our ideas. Through our reports, events and media commentary, we influence today's influencers and decision makers. According to *The Economist*, we're "an organisation that demands attention". We believe Christianity can contribute to the common good and that faith, given space in the public square, will help the UK to flourish.

6

Will you partner with us?

Theos receives no government, corporate or denominational funding. We rely on donations from individuals and organisations to continue our vital work. Please consider signing up as a Theos Friend or Associate or making a one off donation today.

Theos Friends and Students

— Stay up to date with our monthly newsletter

— Receive (free) printed copies of our reports

— Get free tickets to all our events

£75/ year
for Friends

£40/ year
for Students

Theos Associates

— Stay up to date with our monthly newsletter

— Receive (free) printed copies of our reports

— Get free tickets to all our events

— Get invites to private events with the Theos team and other Theos Associates

£375/ year

Sign up on our website:
www.theosthinktank.co.uk/about/support-us